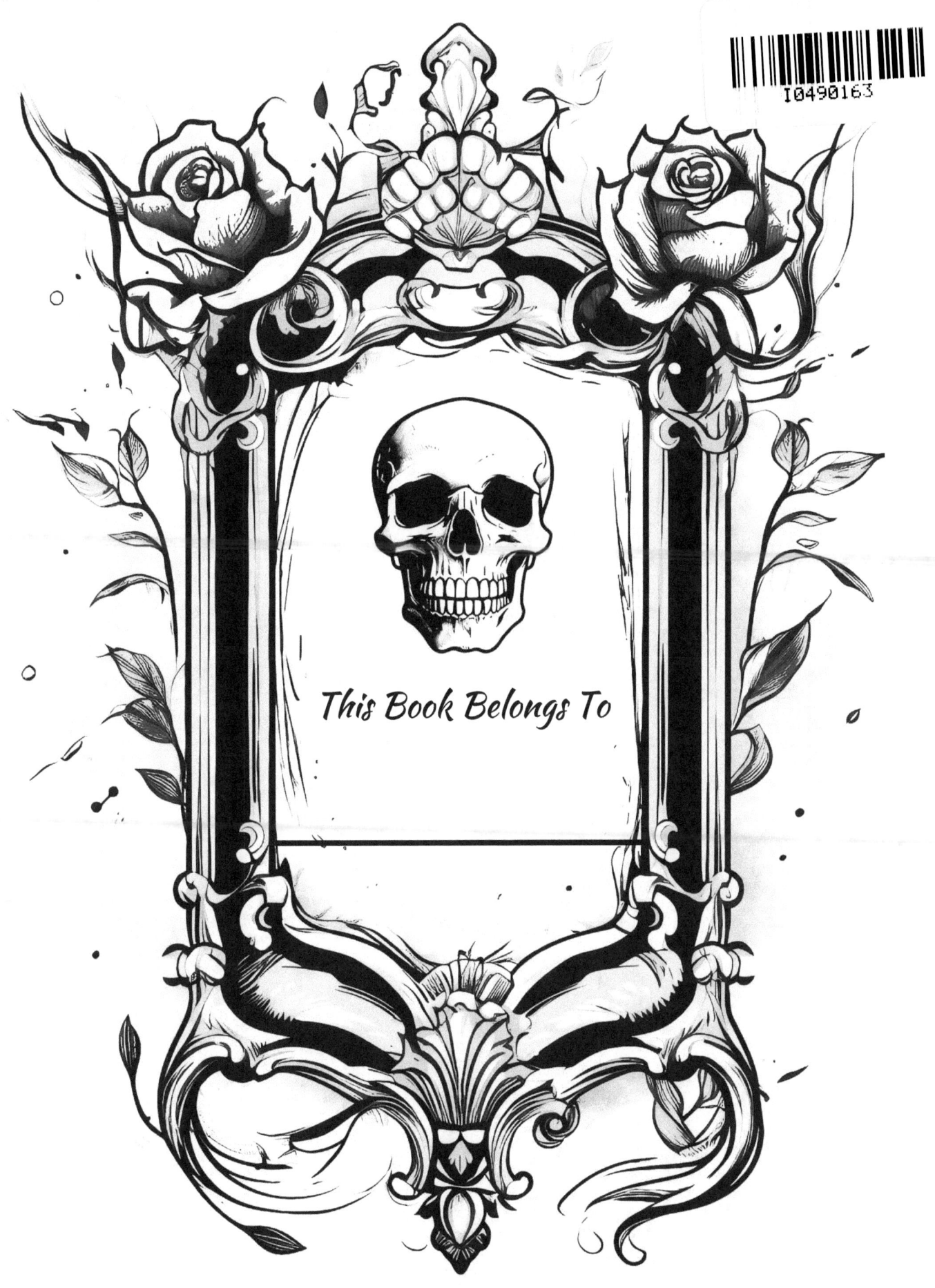

This Book Belongs To

Anchor

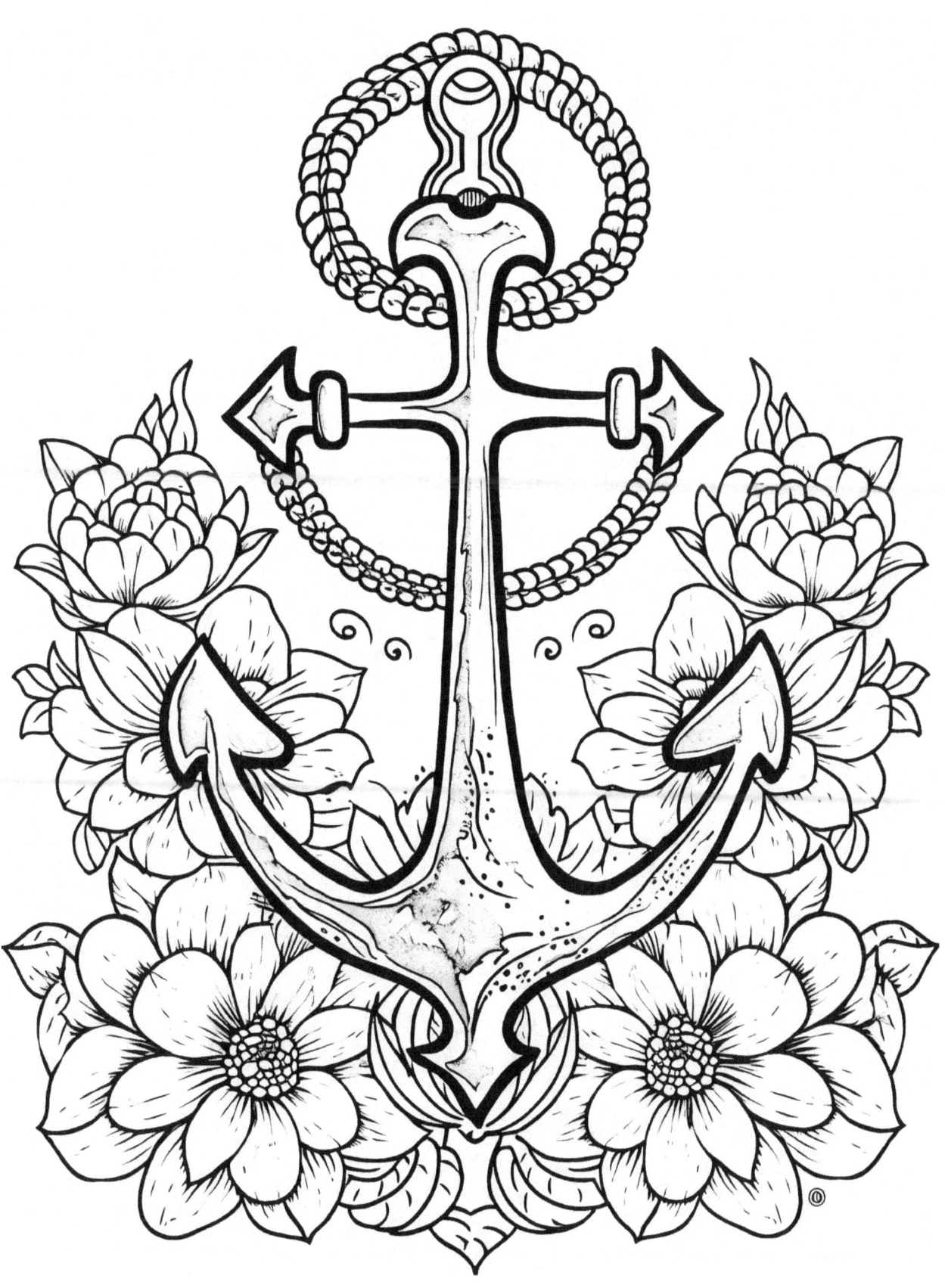

Arrow

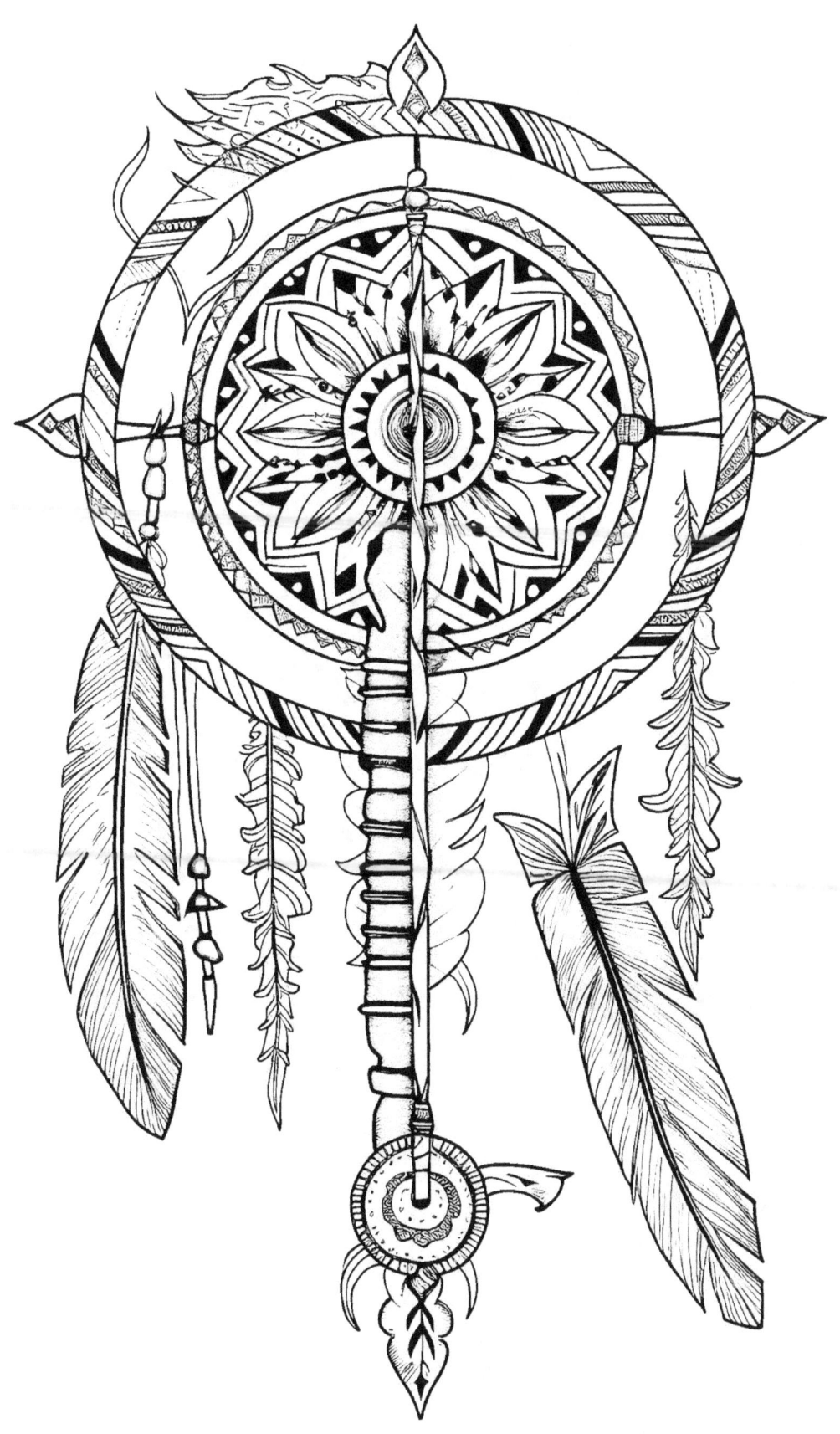

Books

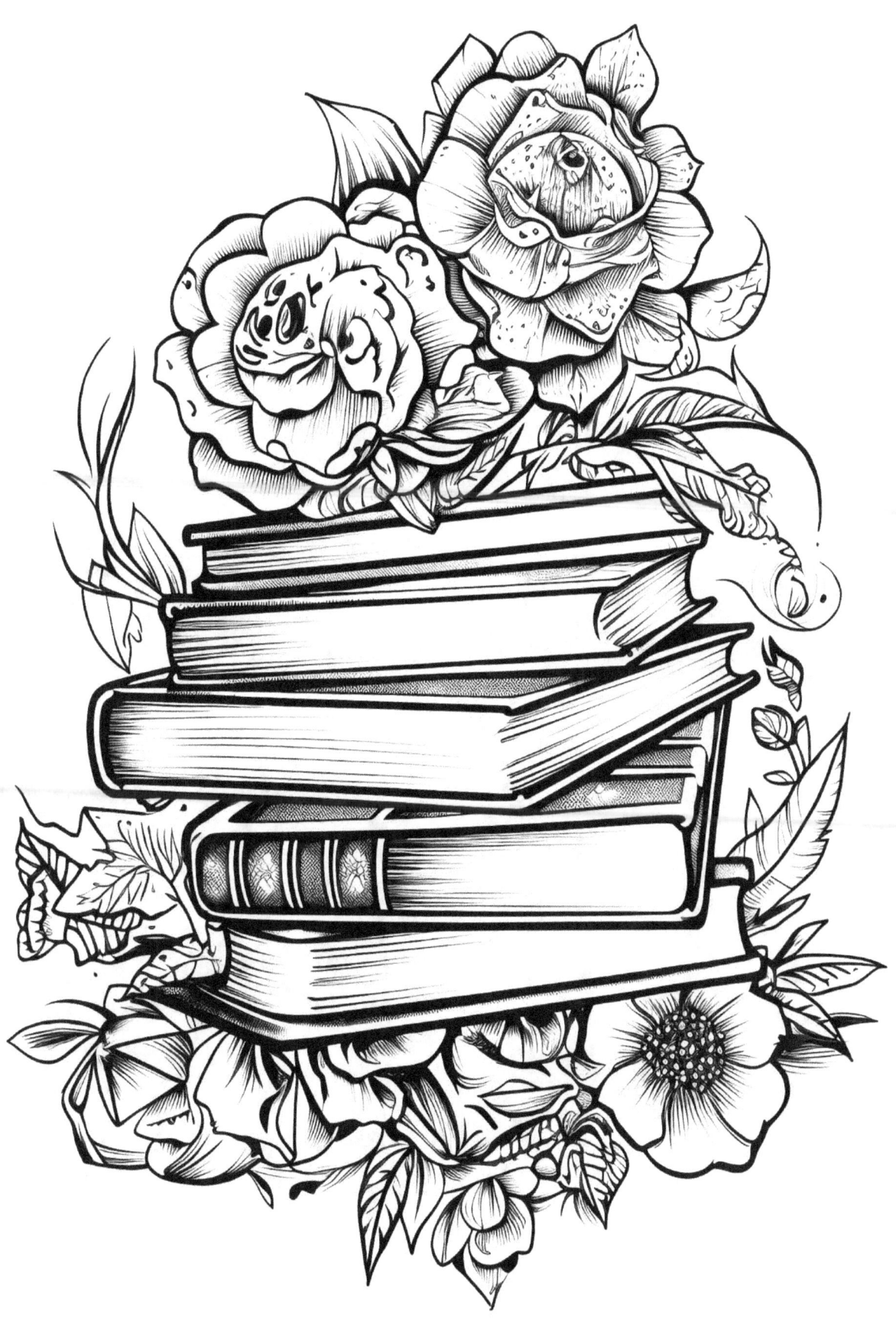

Butterfly

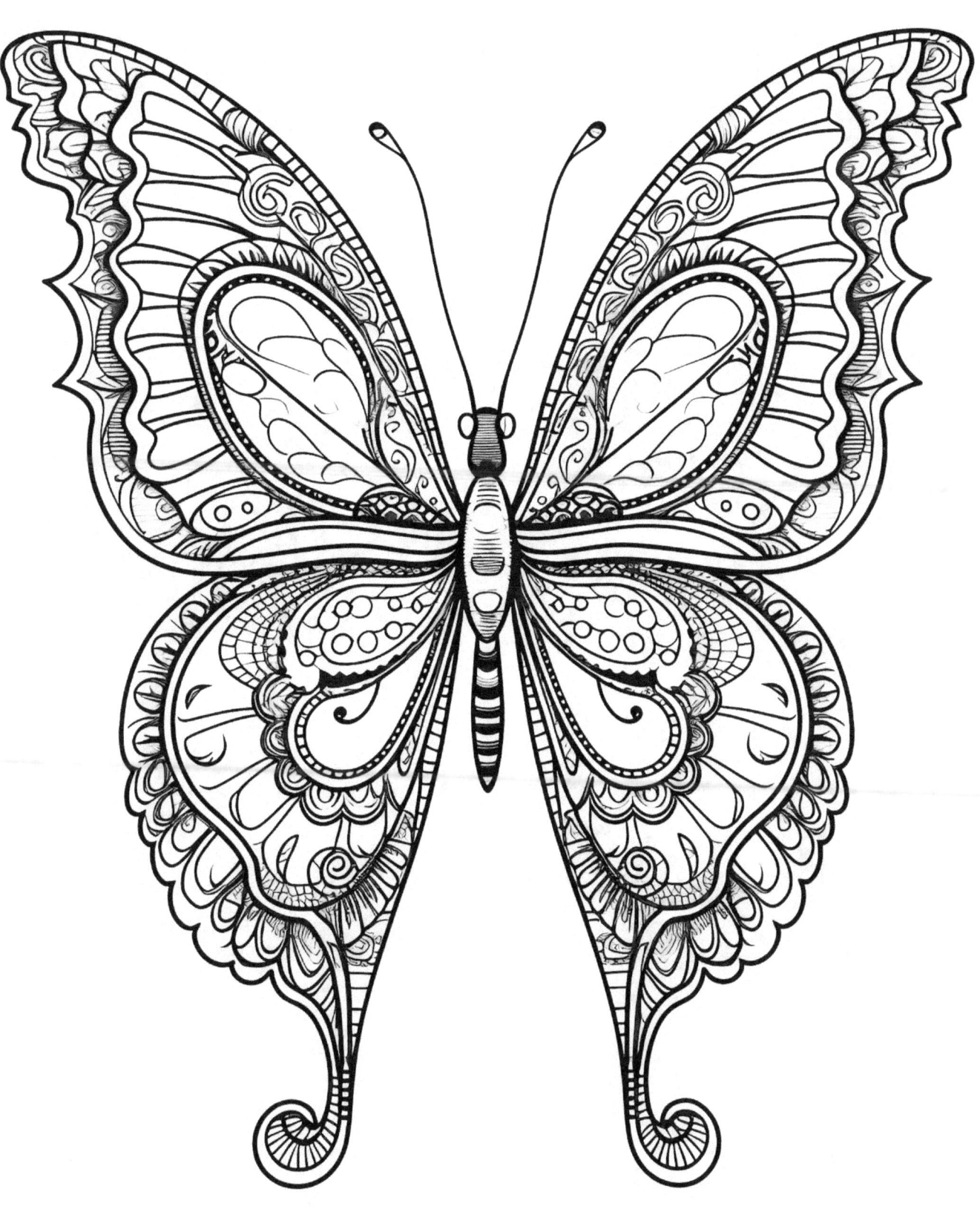

Cactus

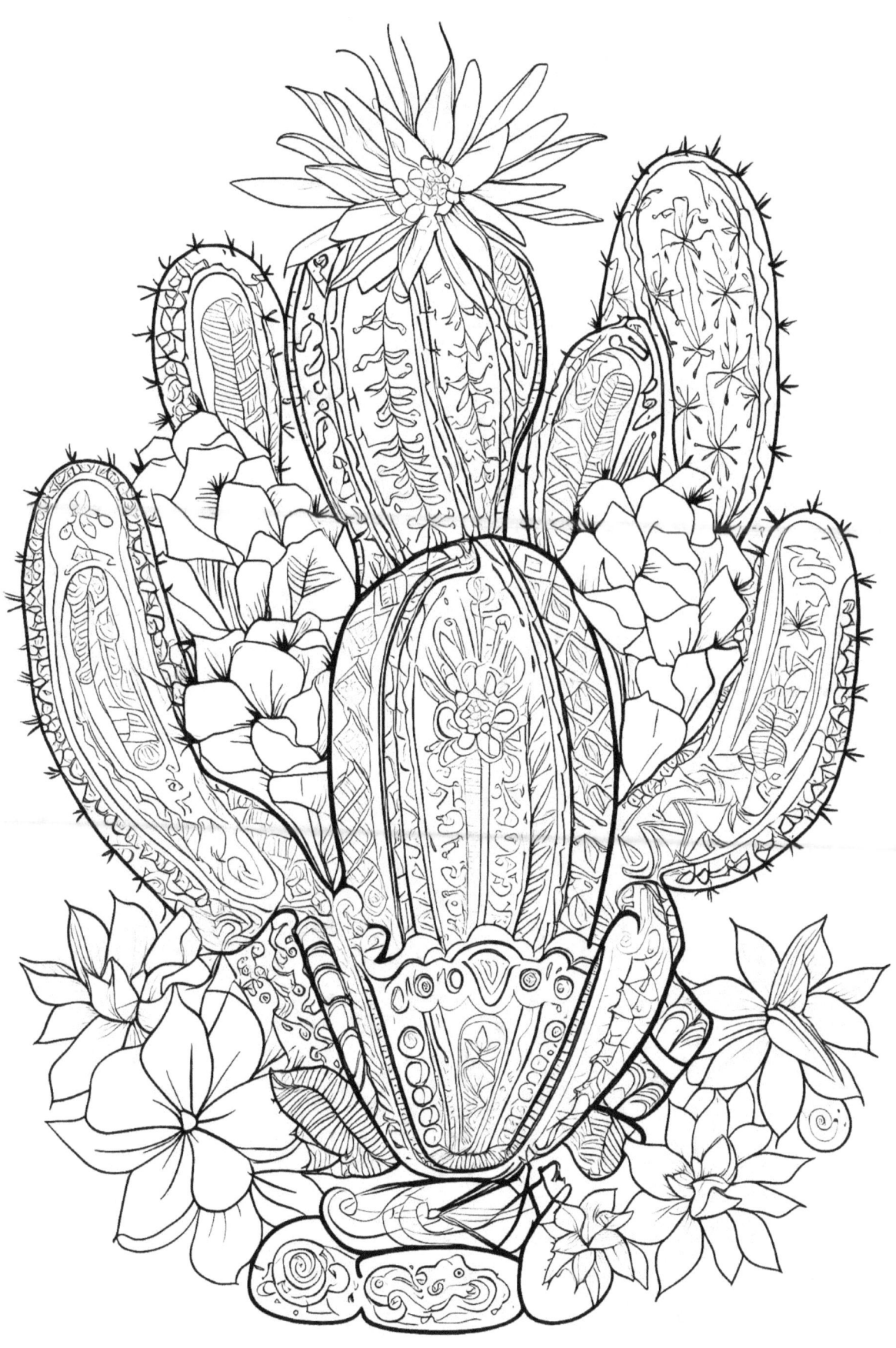

Compass

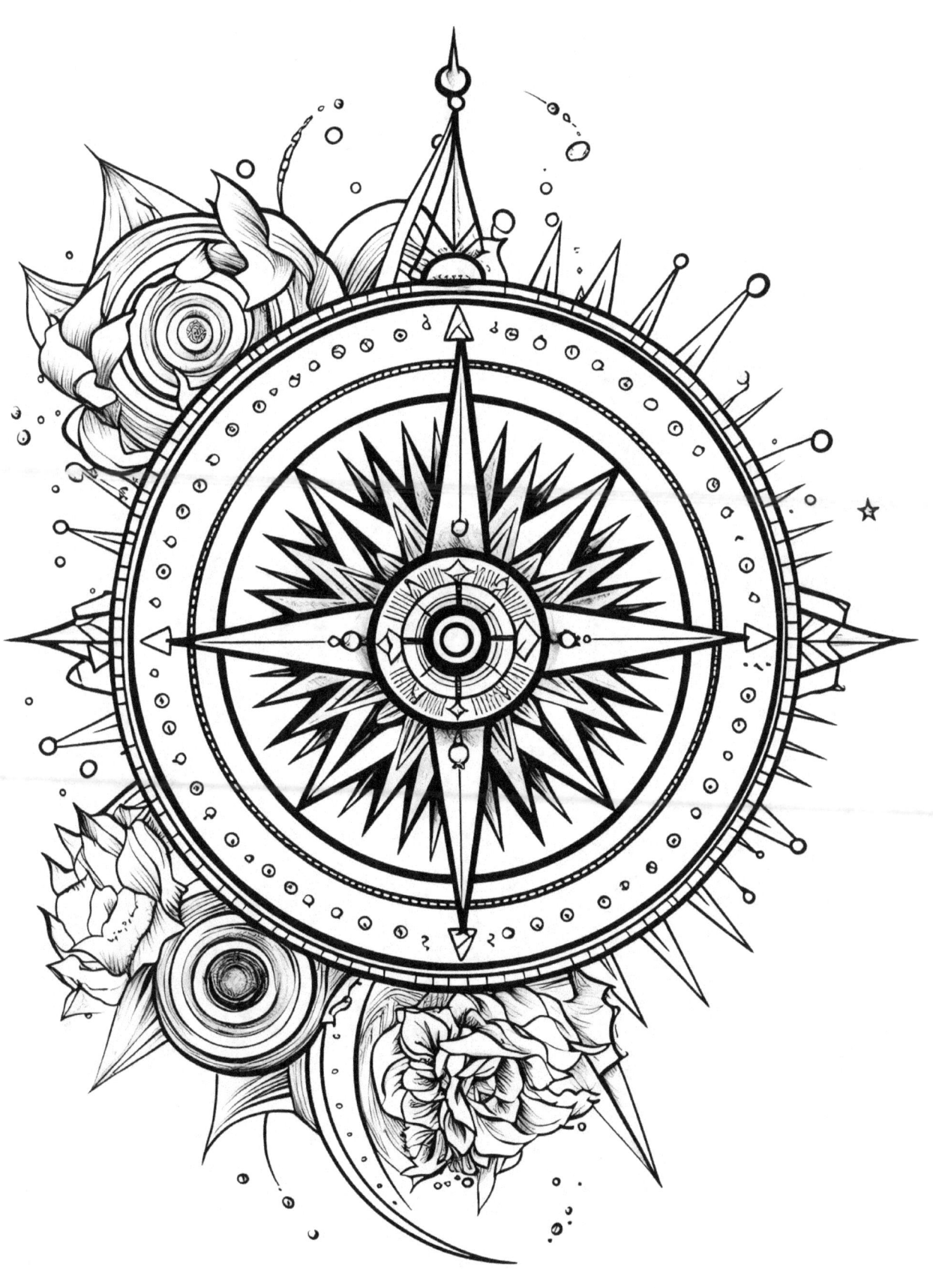

Cross

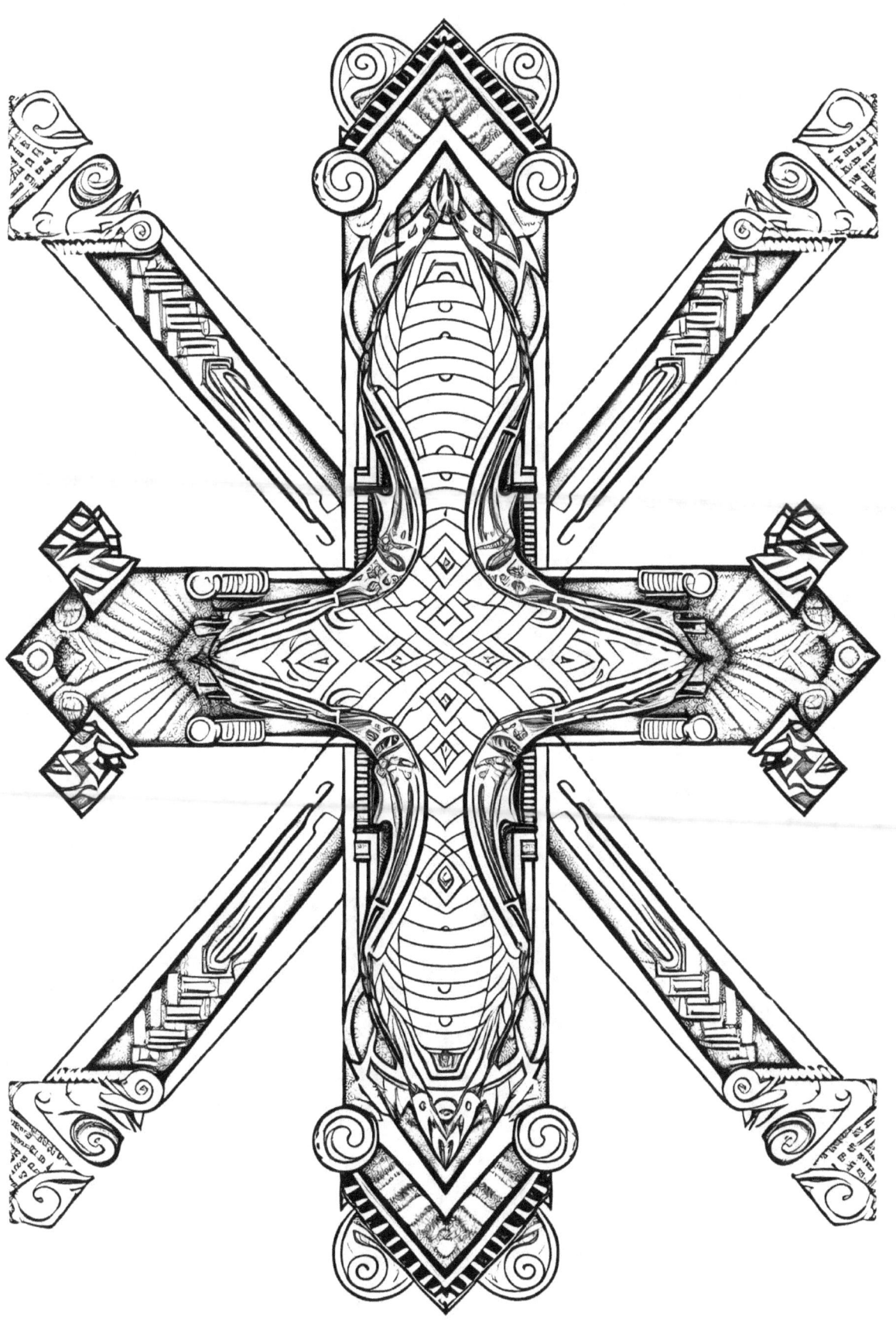

Crown

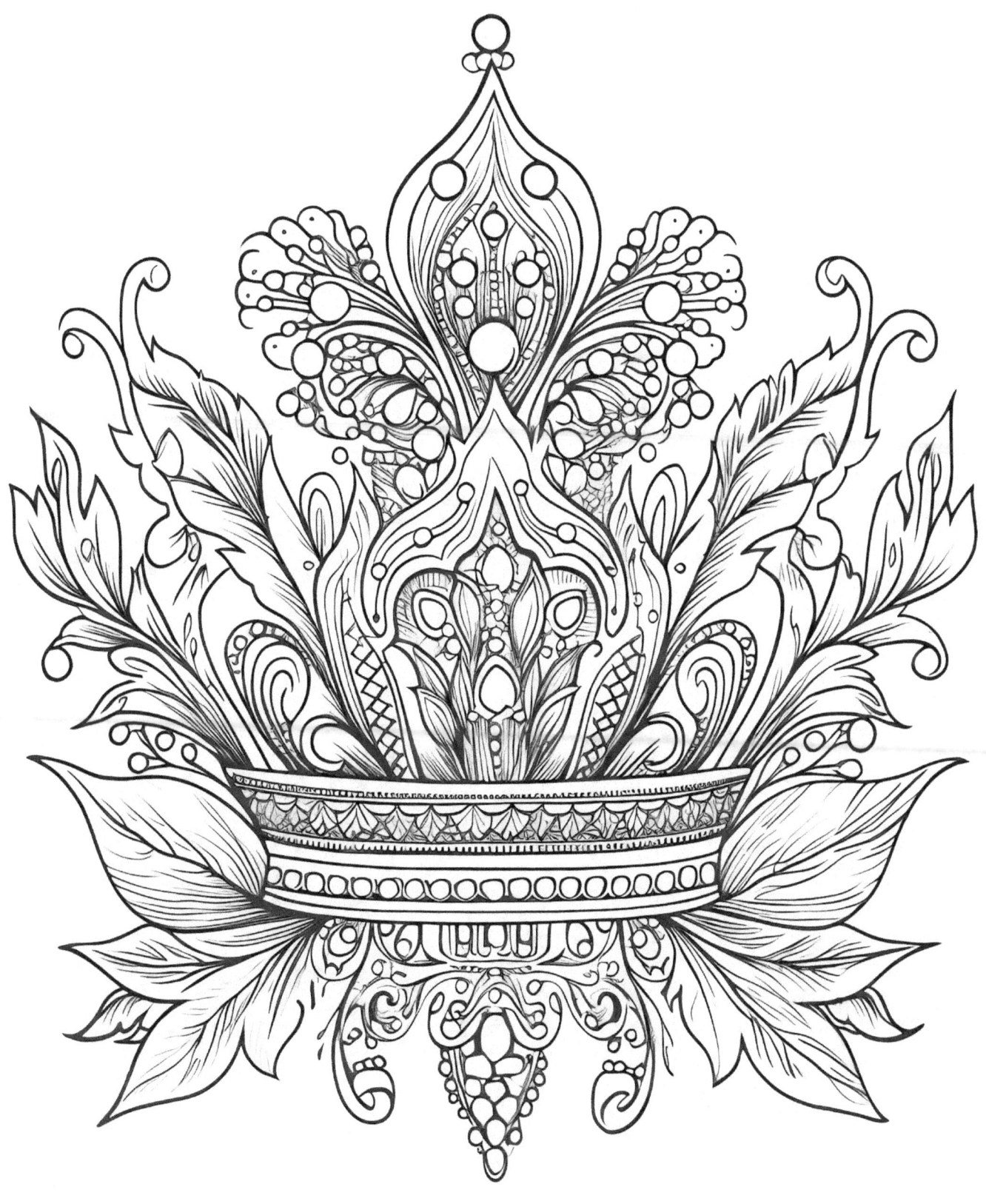

Diamond

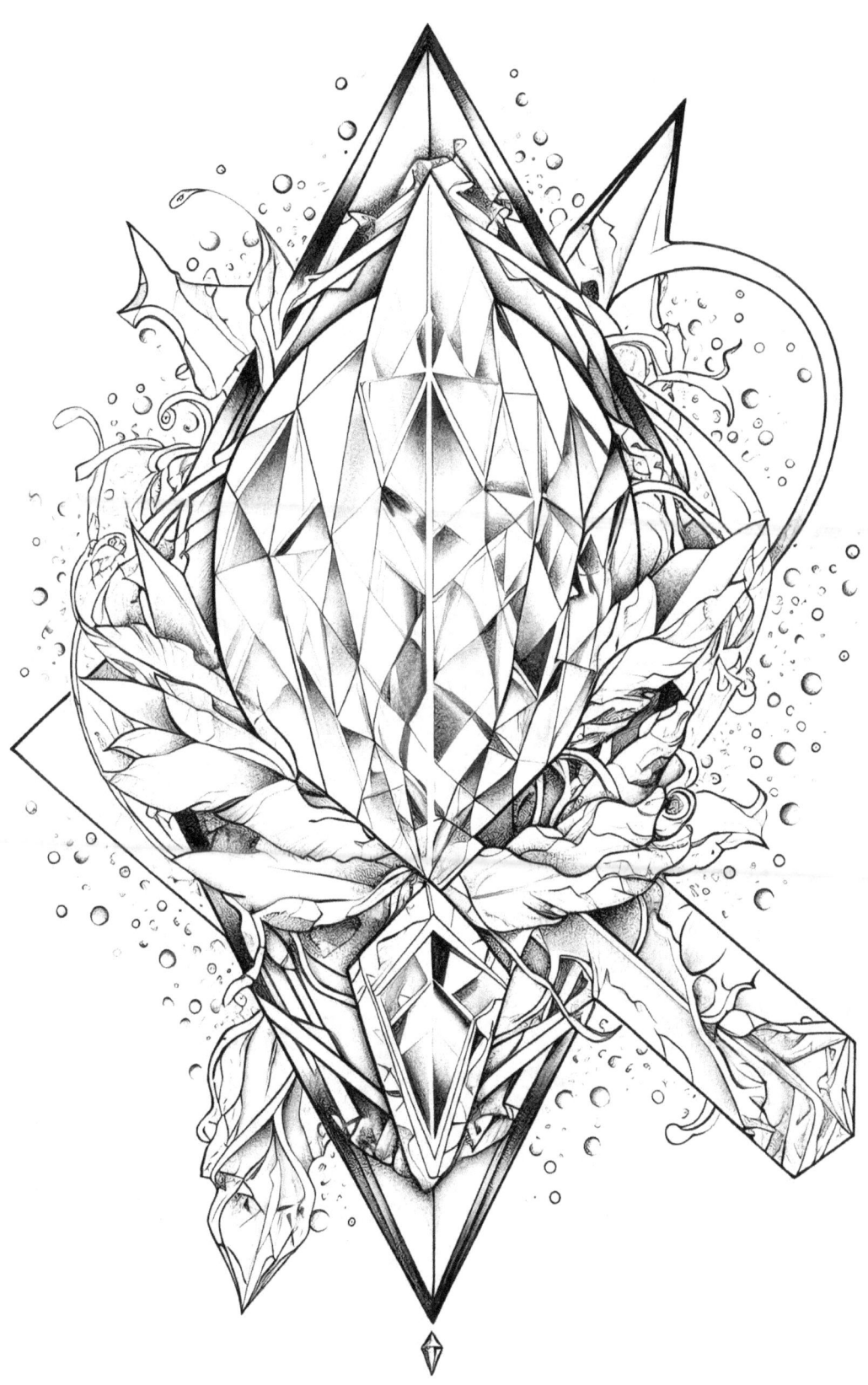

Dinosaur

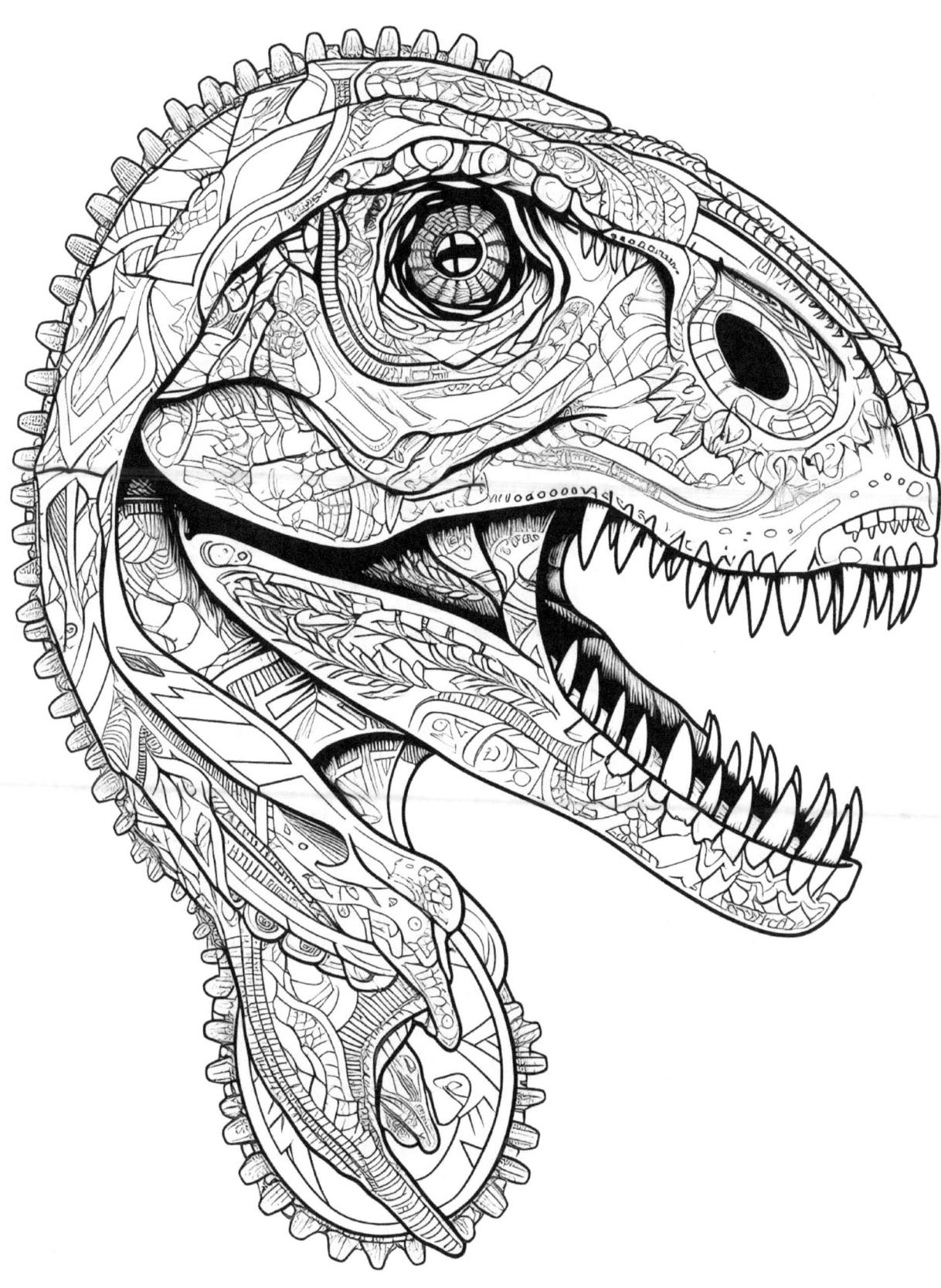

Dolphin

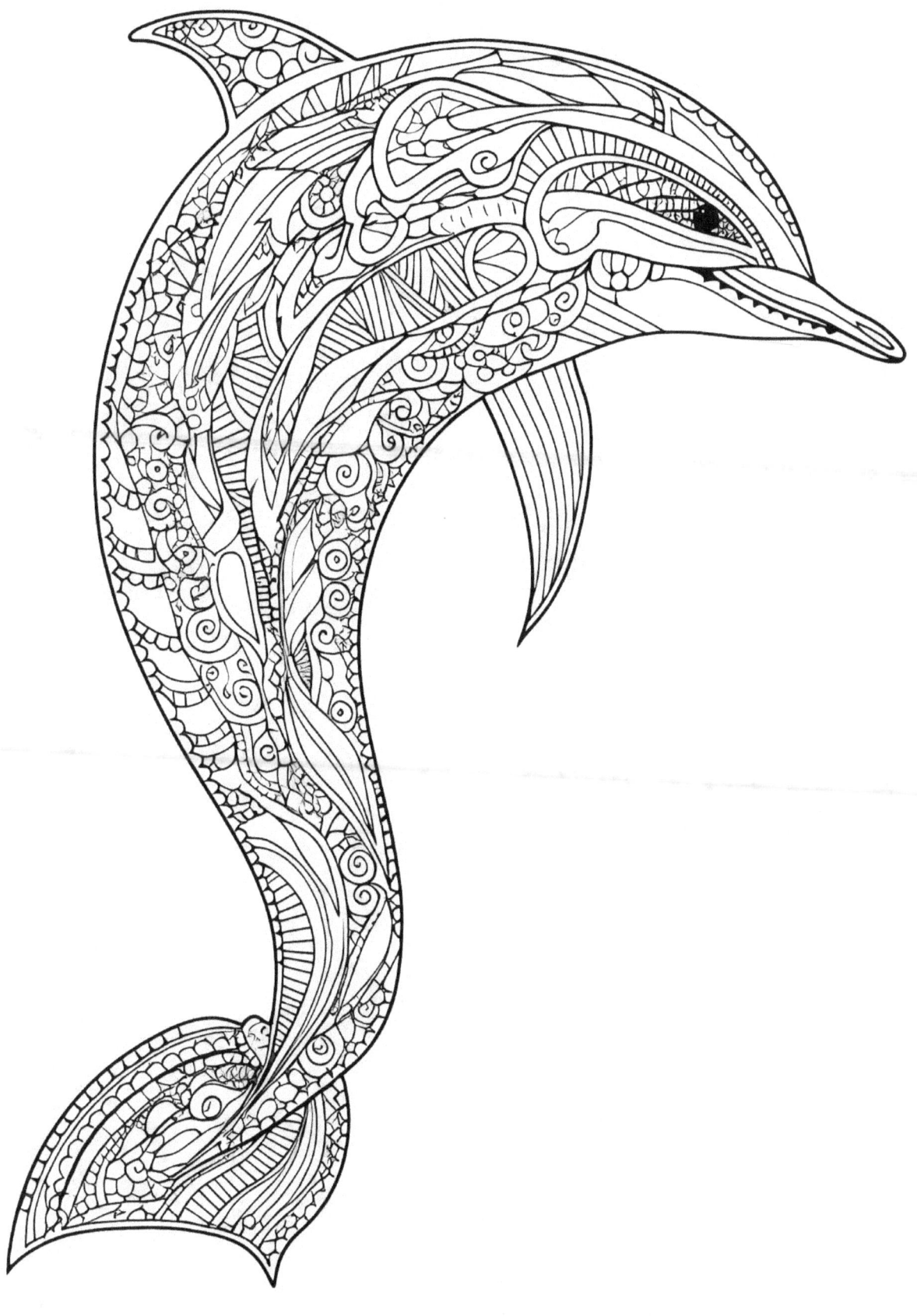

Dragon

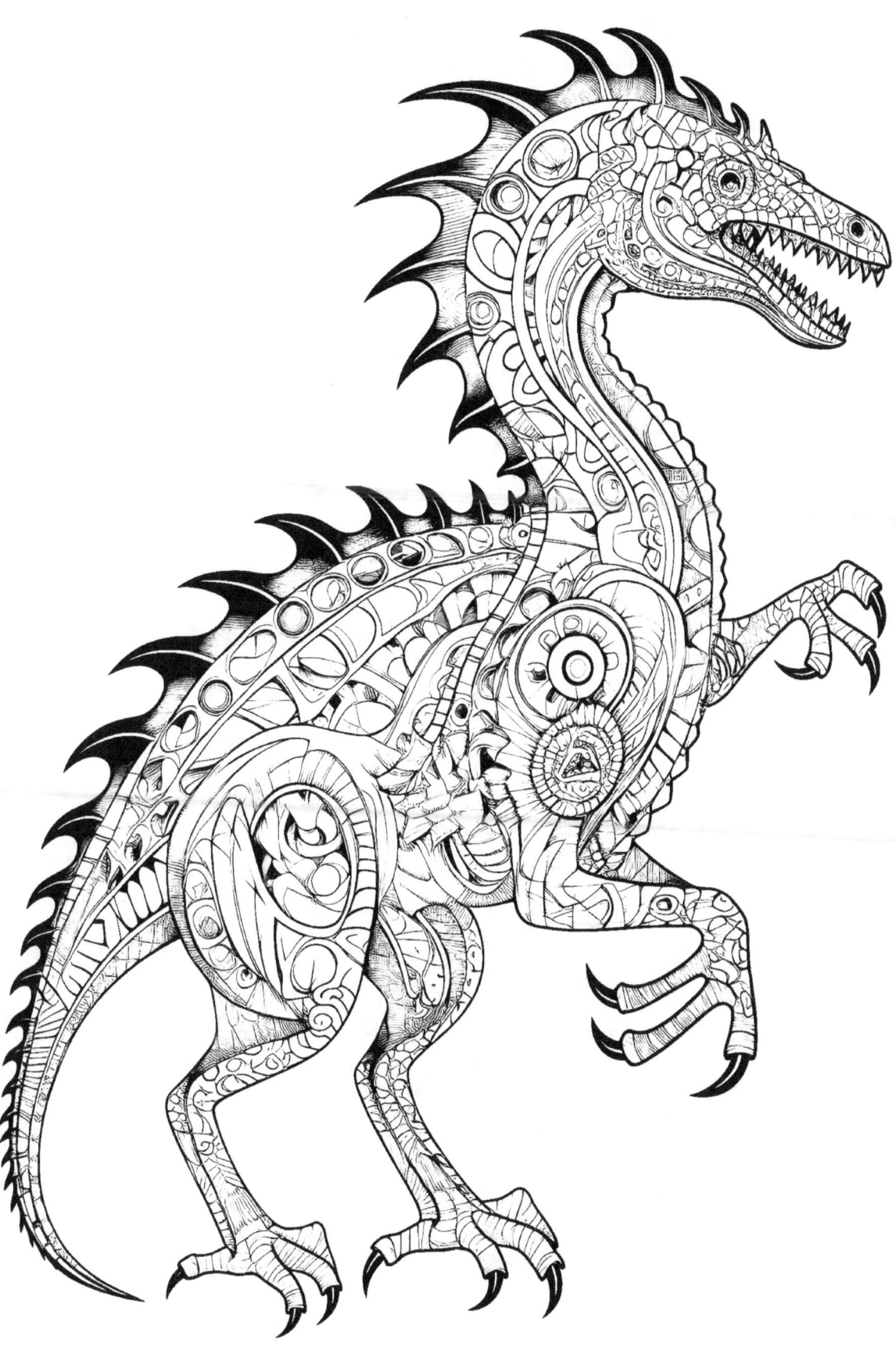

Eye

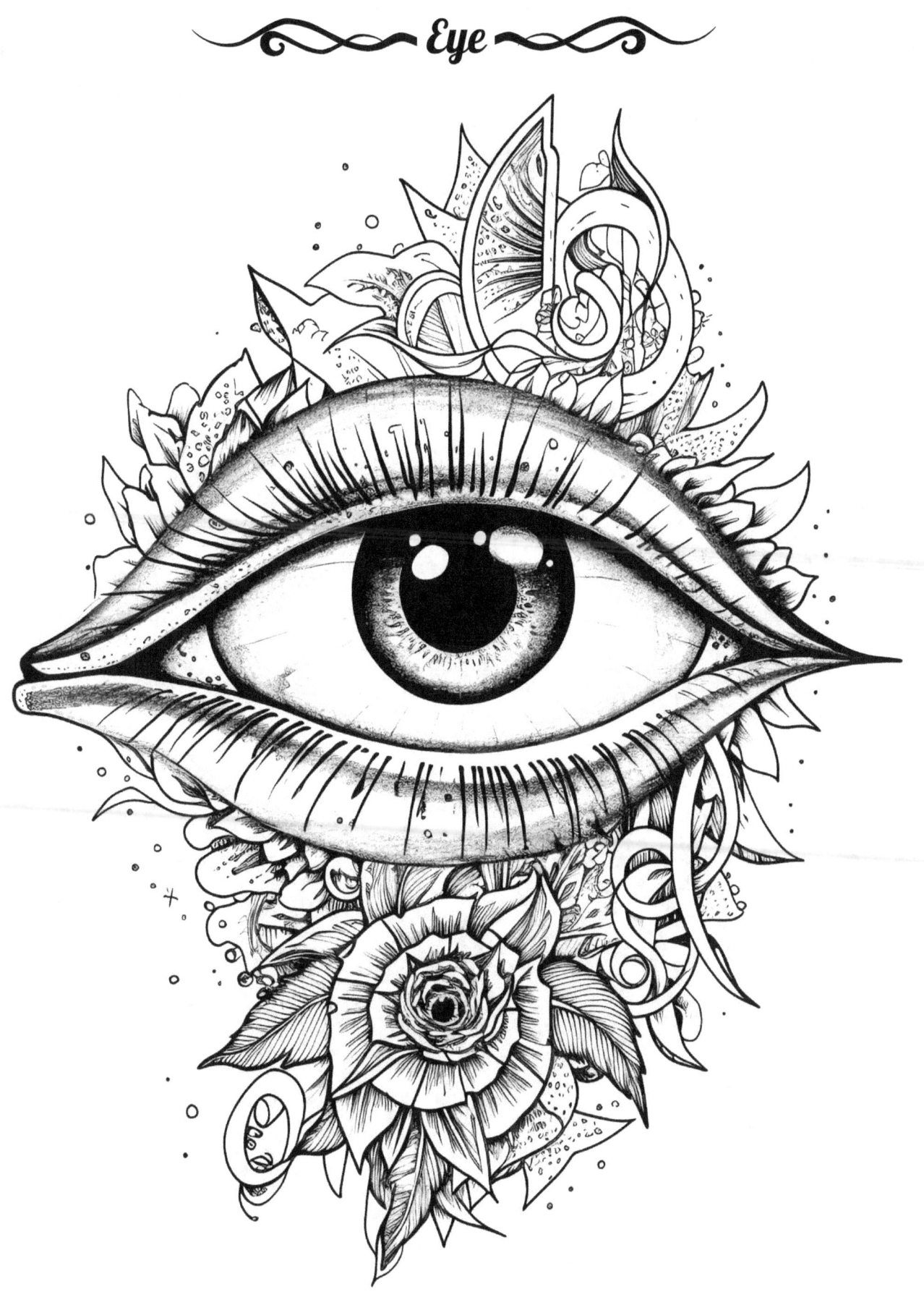

Growing Tree

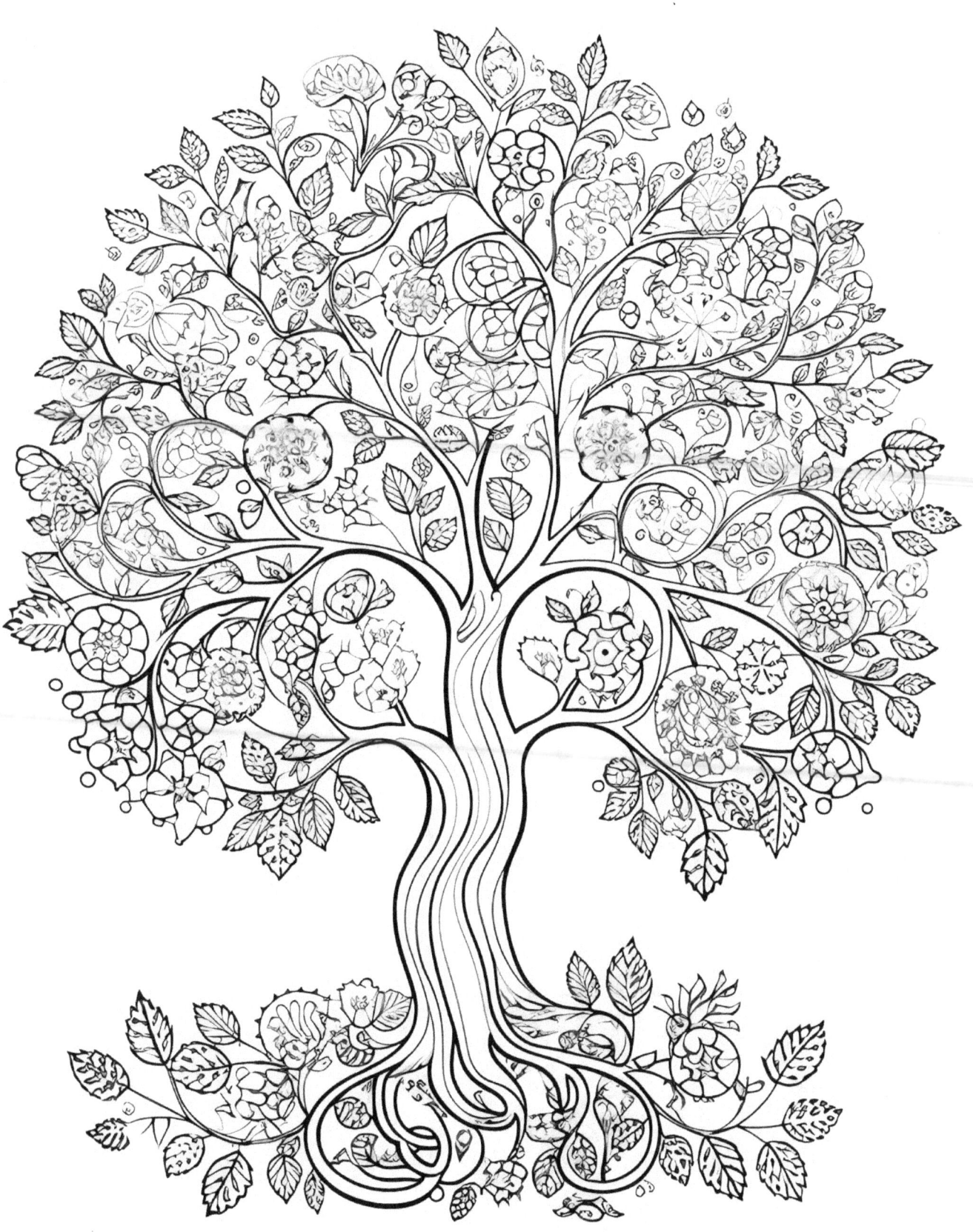

Heart

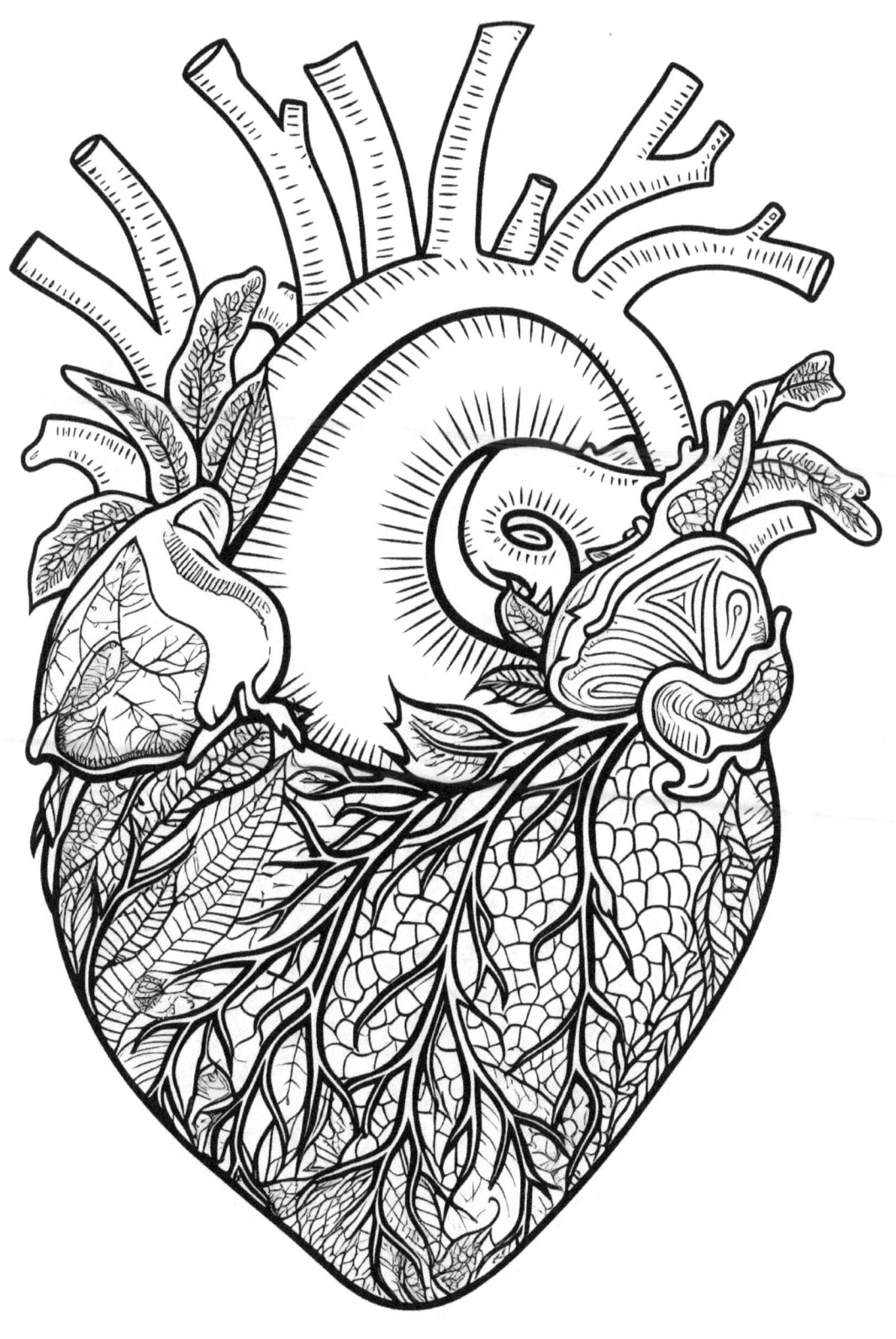

Key

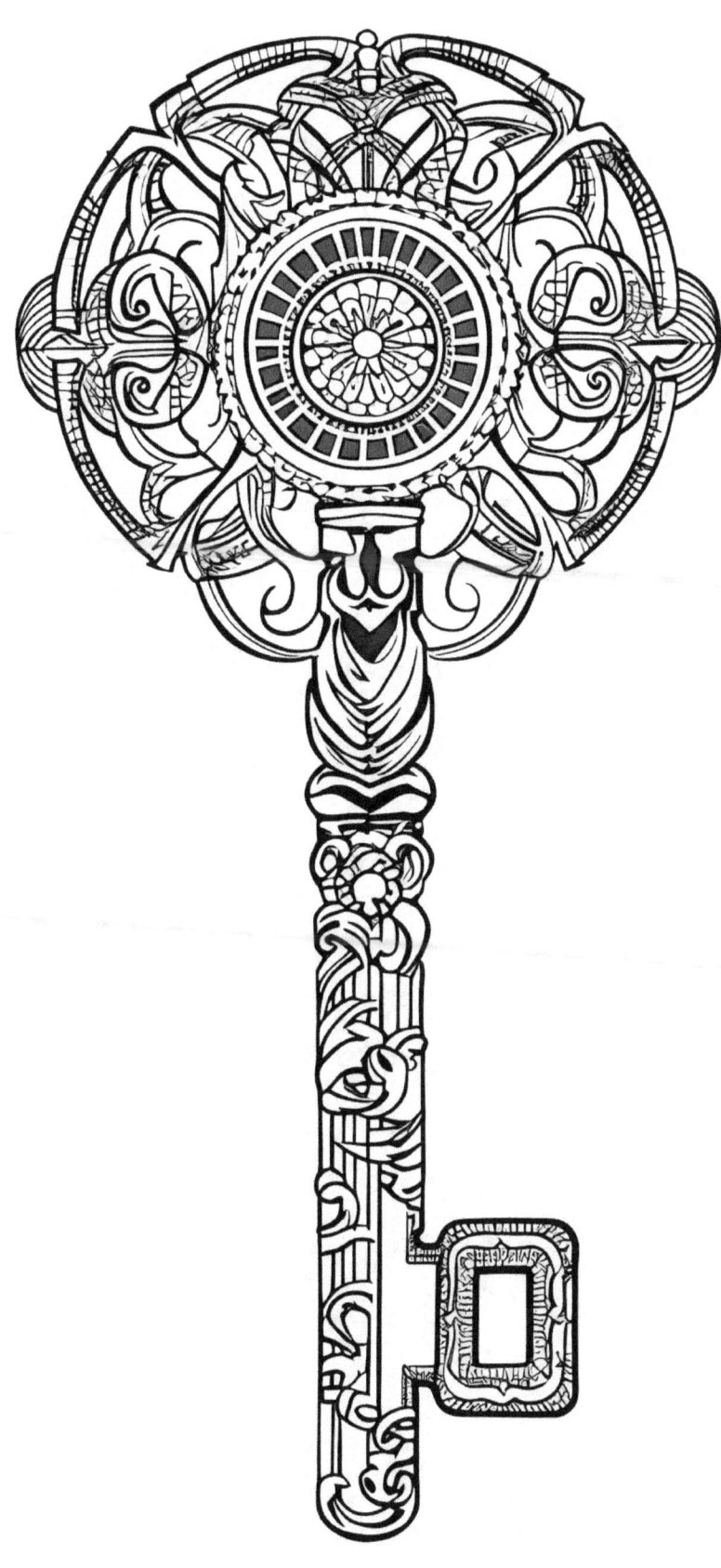

Ladybug

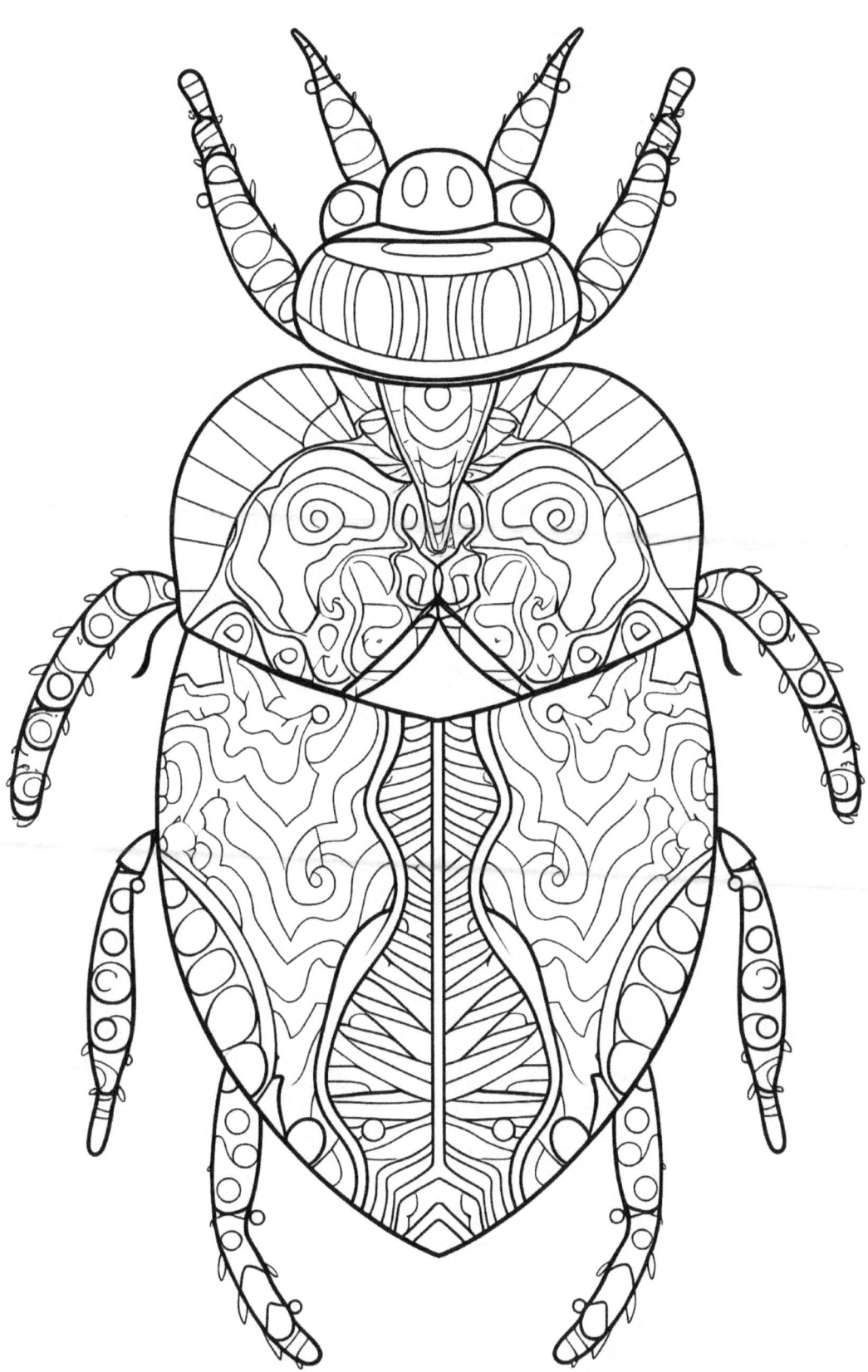

Leafy Branch

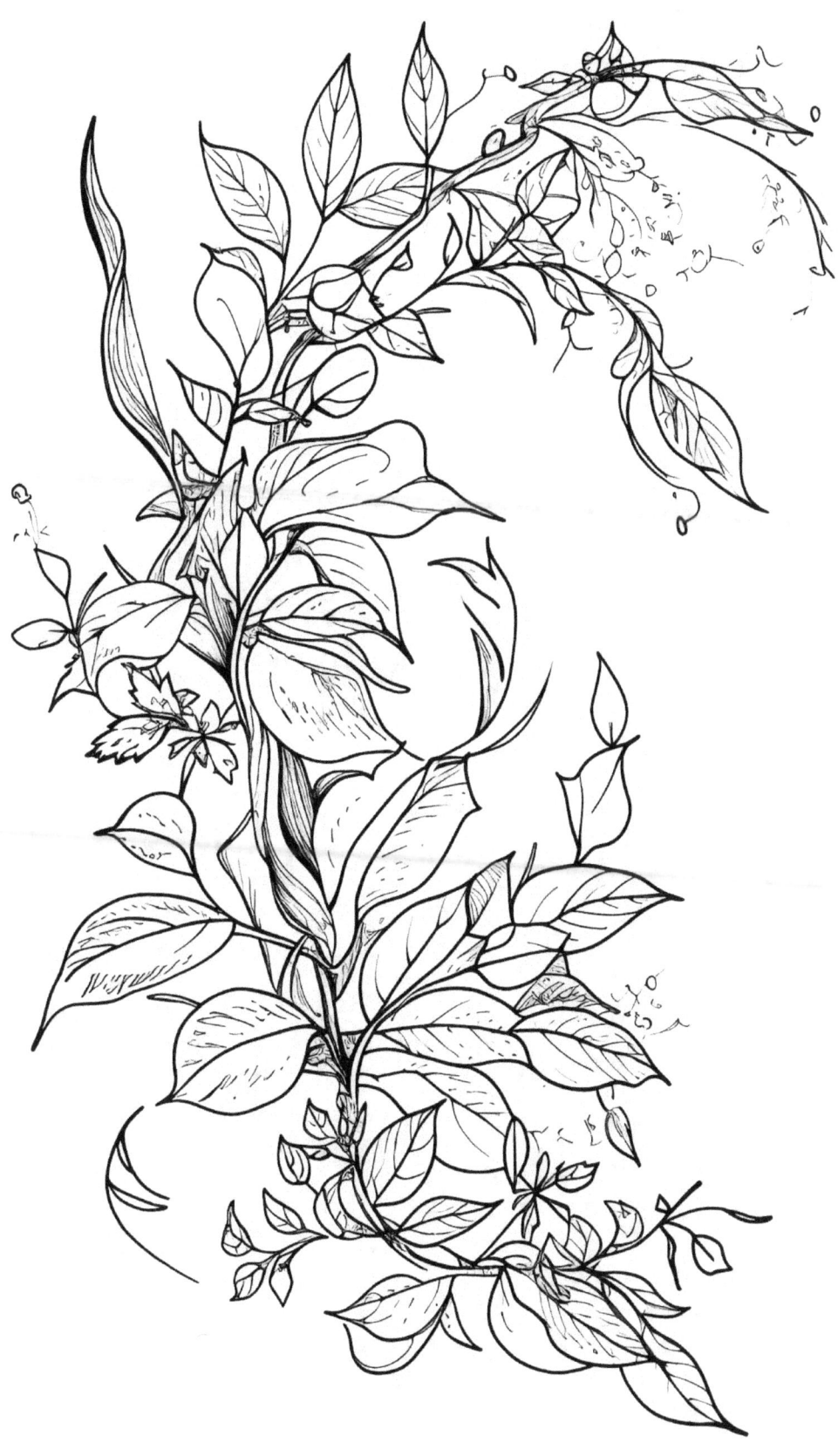

Lightning Bolt

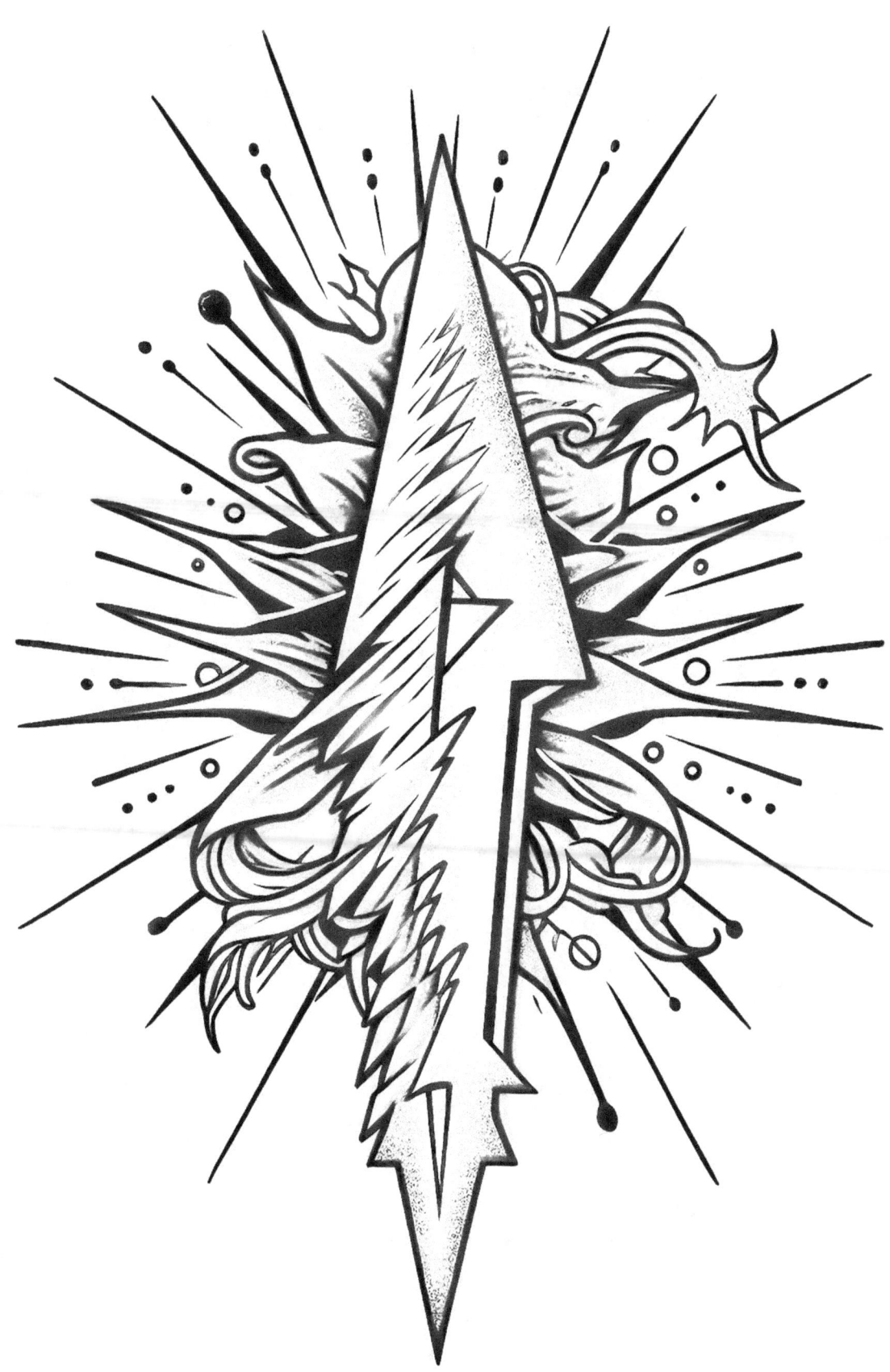

Lion

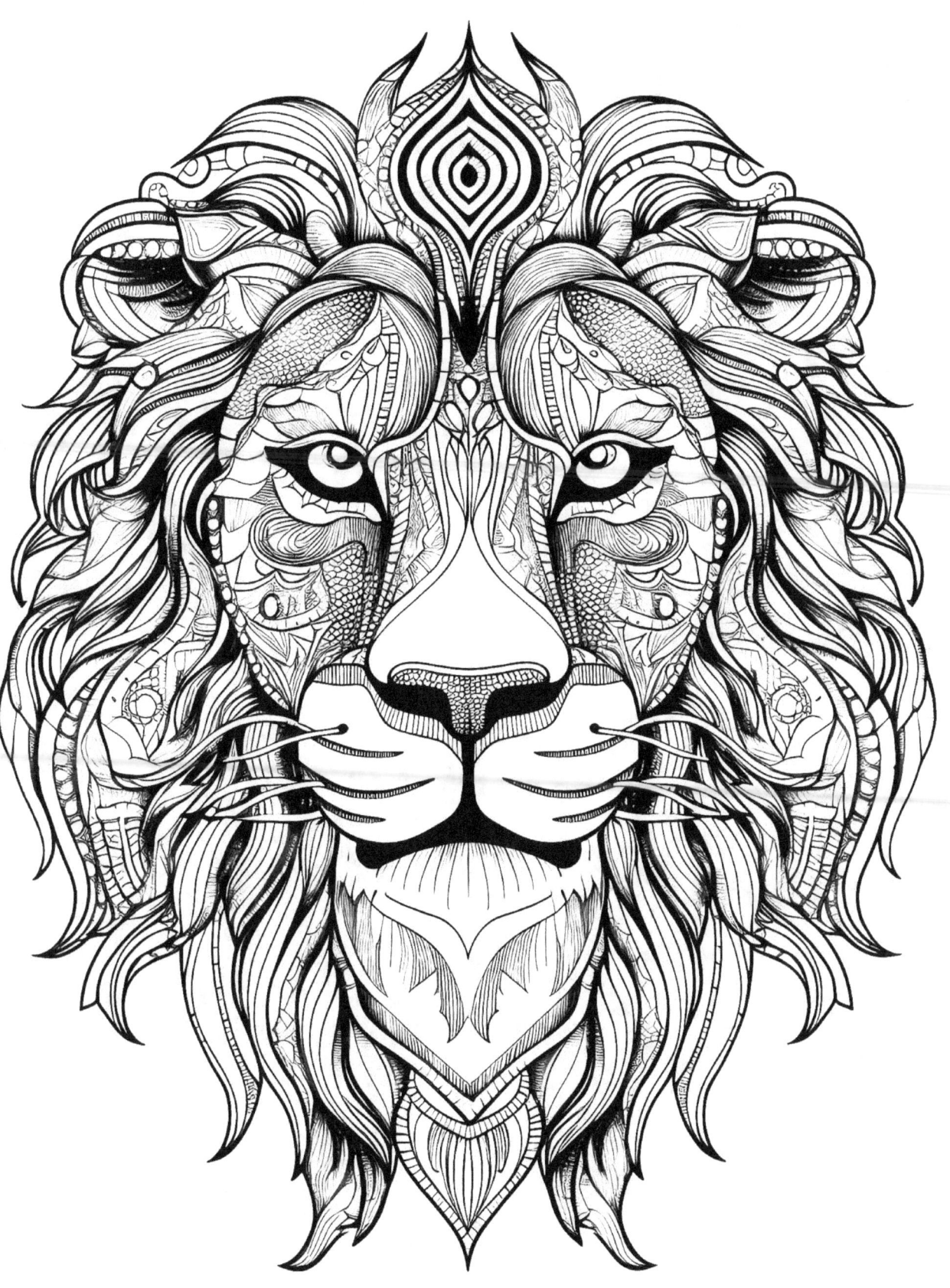

Lotus Flower

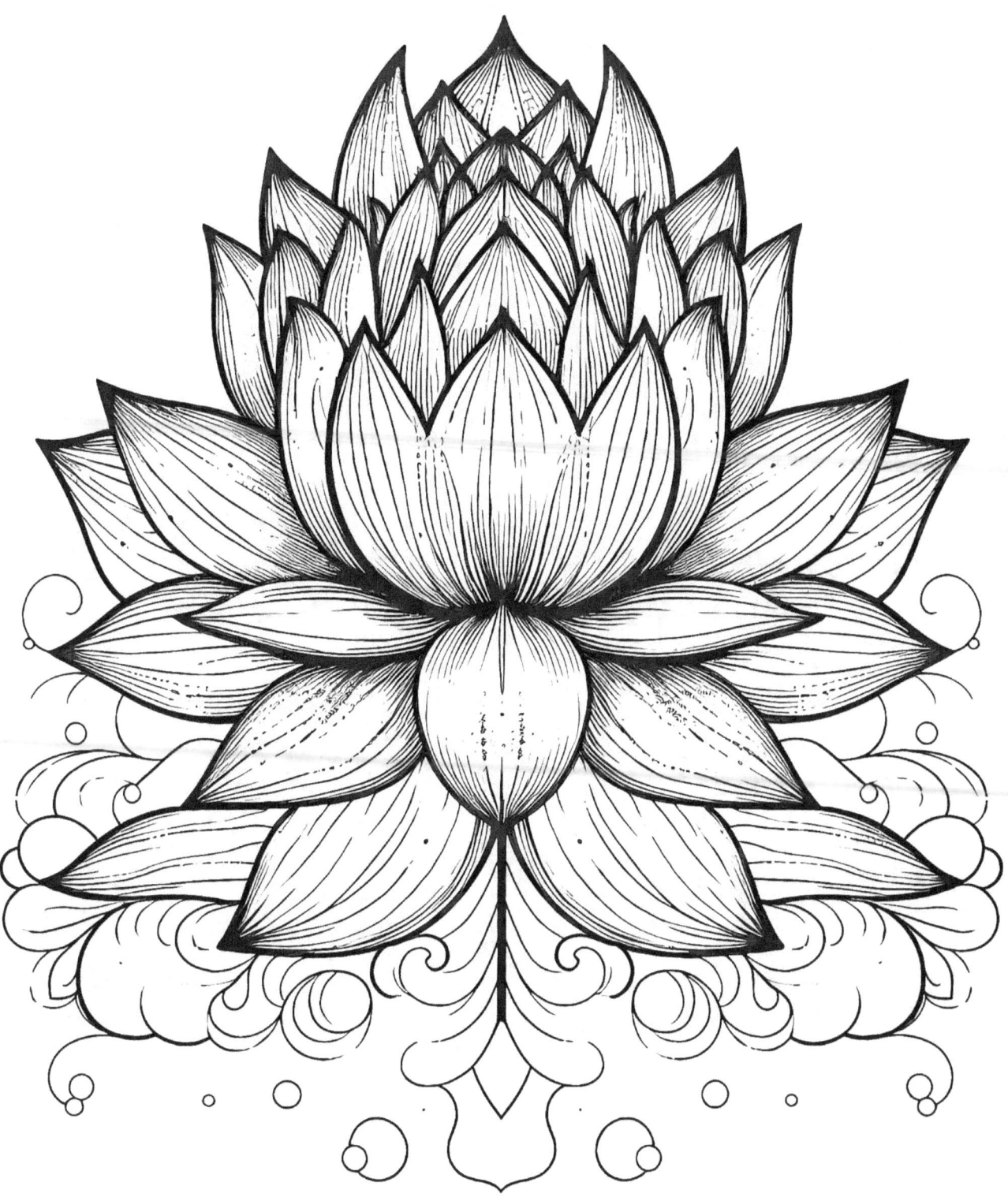

Maple Leaf

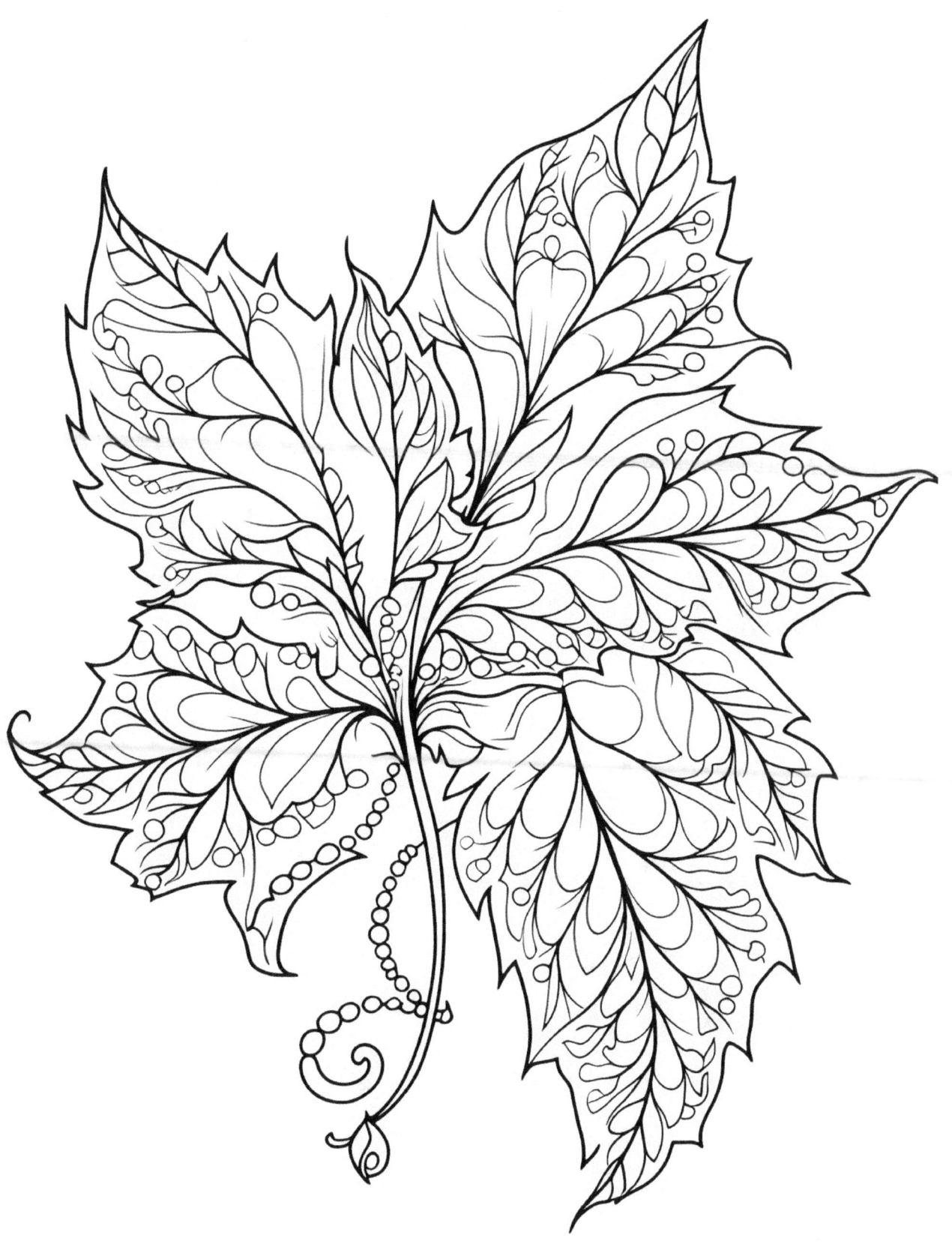

Moon

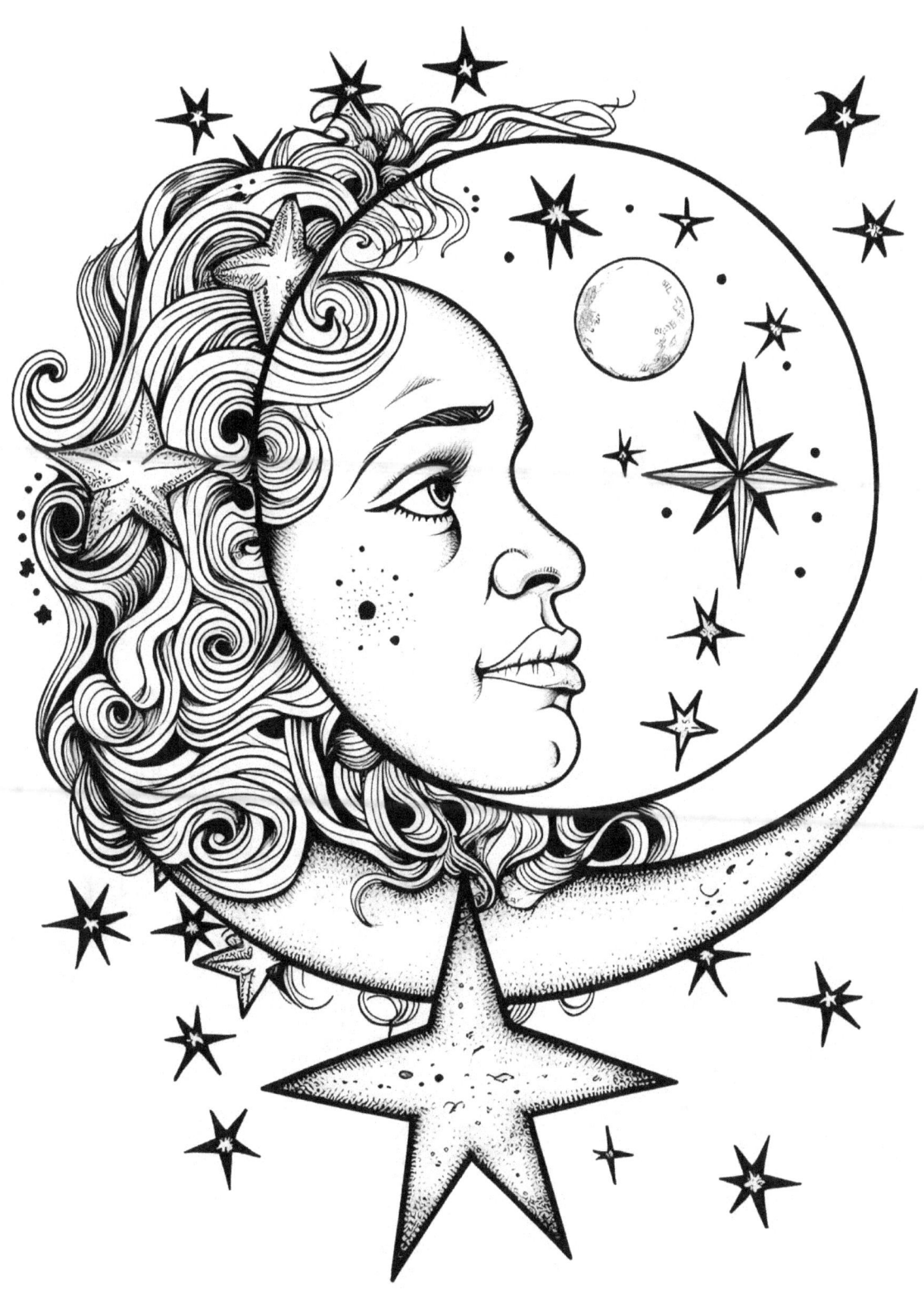

Mountains

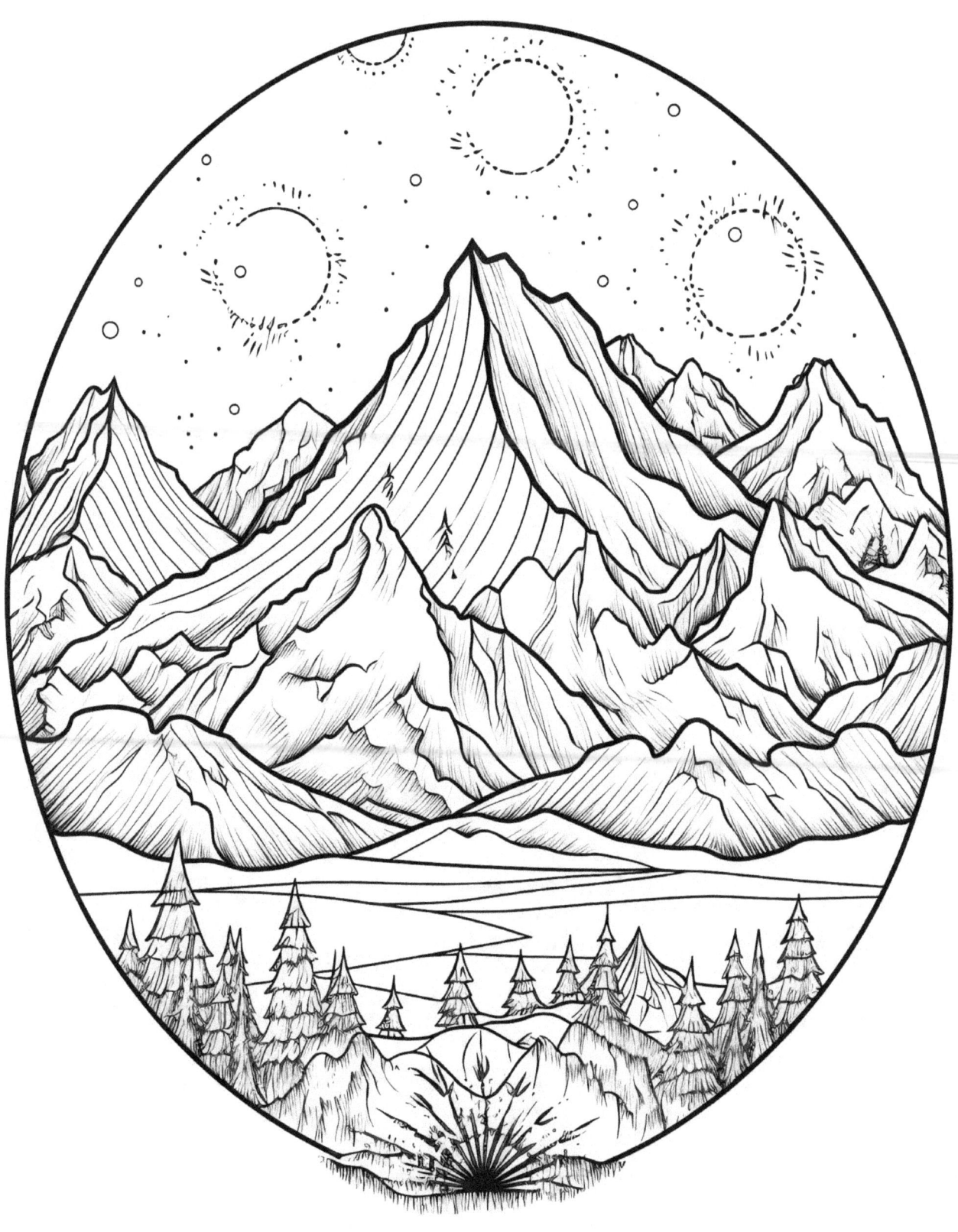

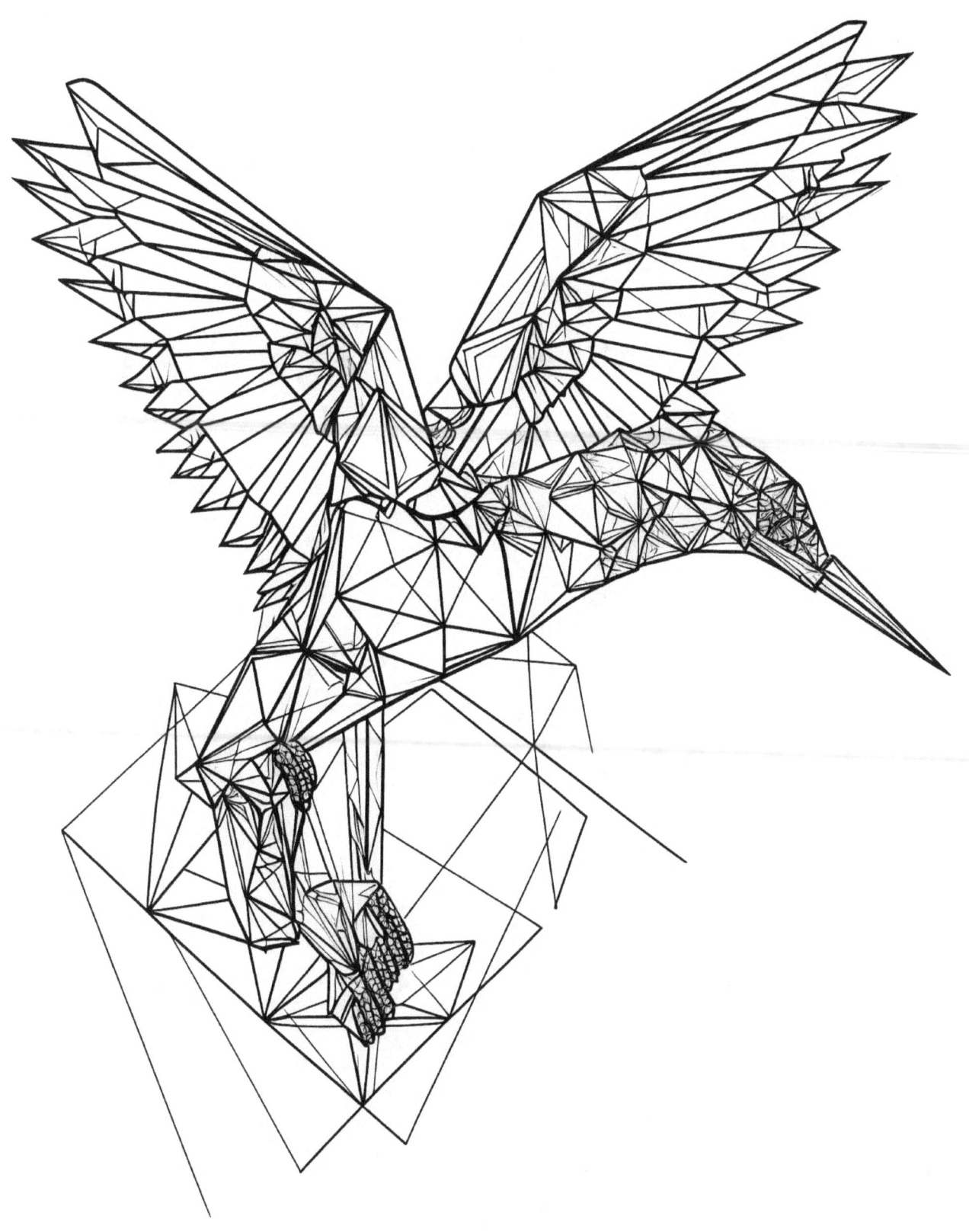

Palm Tree

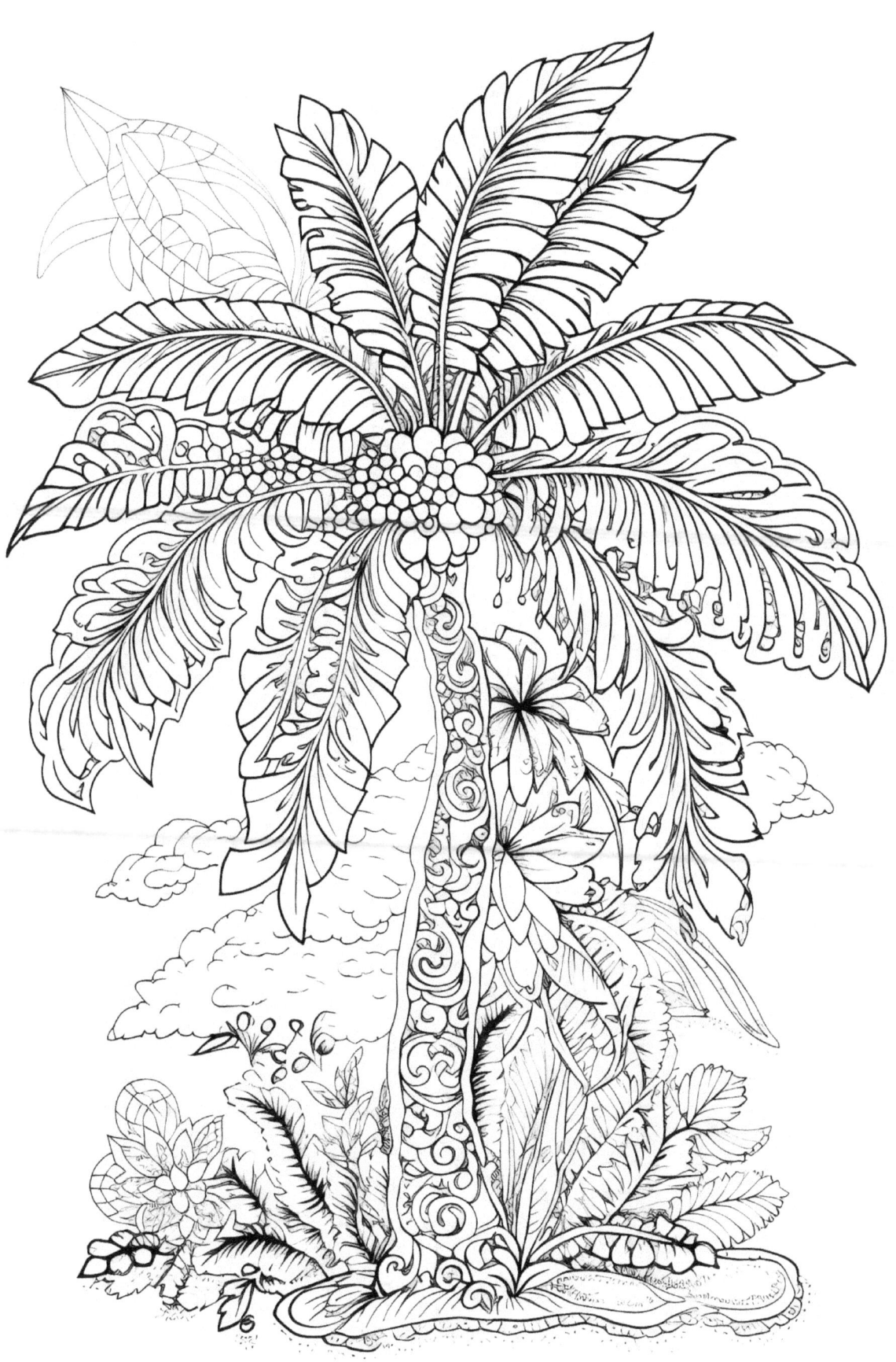

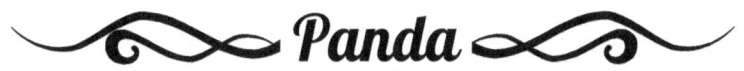

Panda

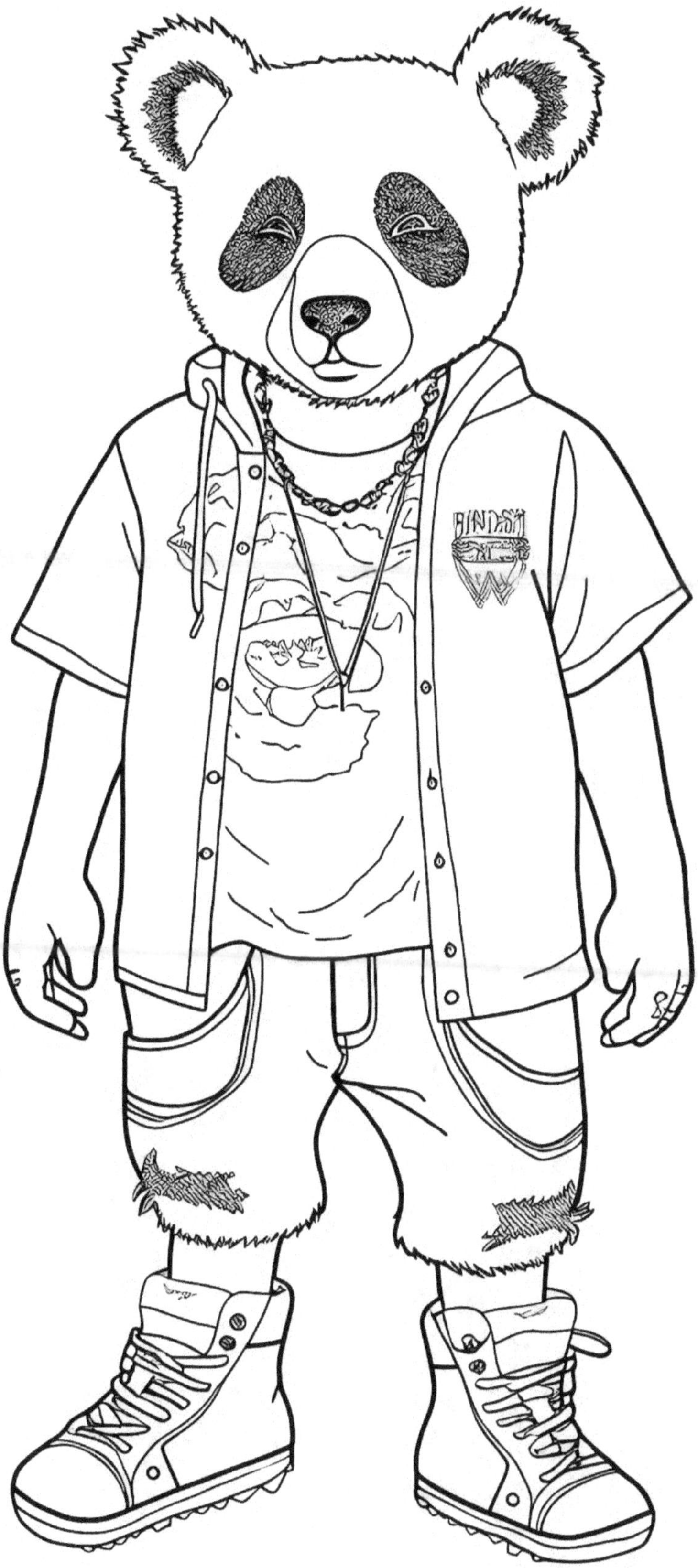

Plant

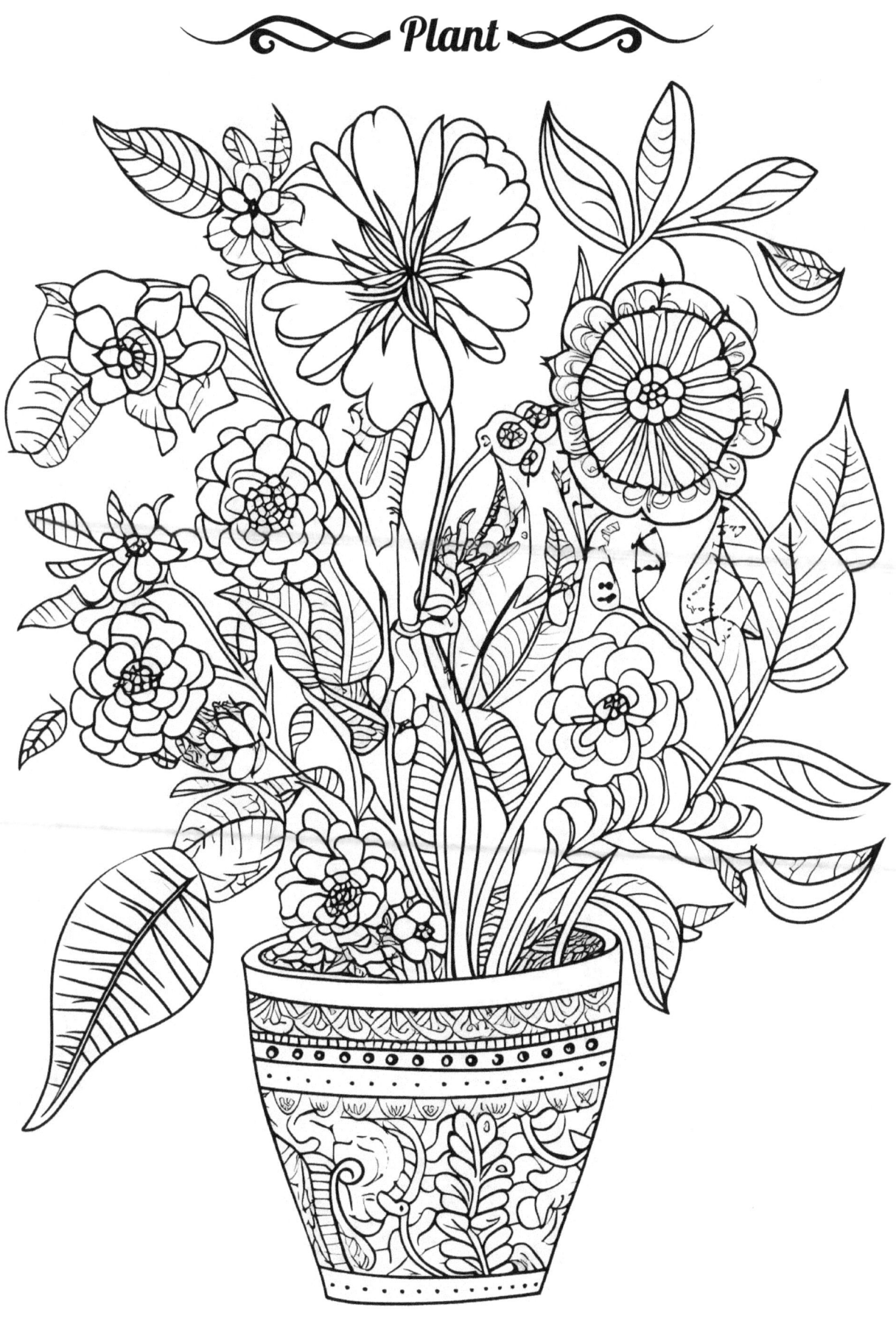

Raven

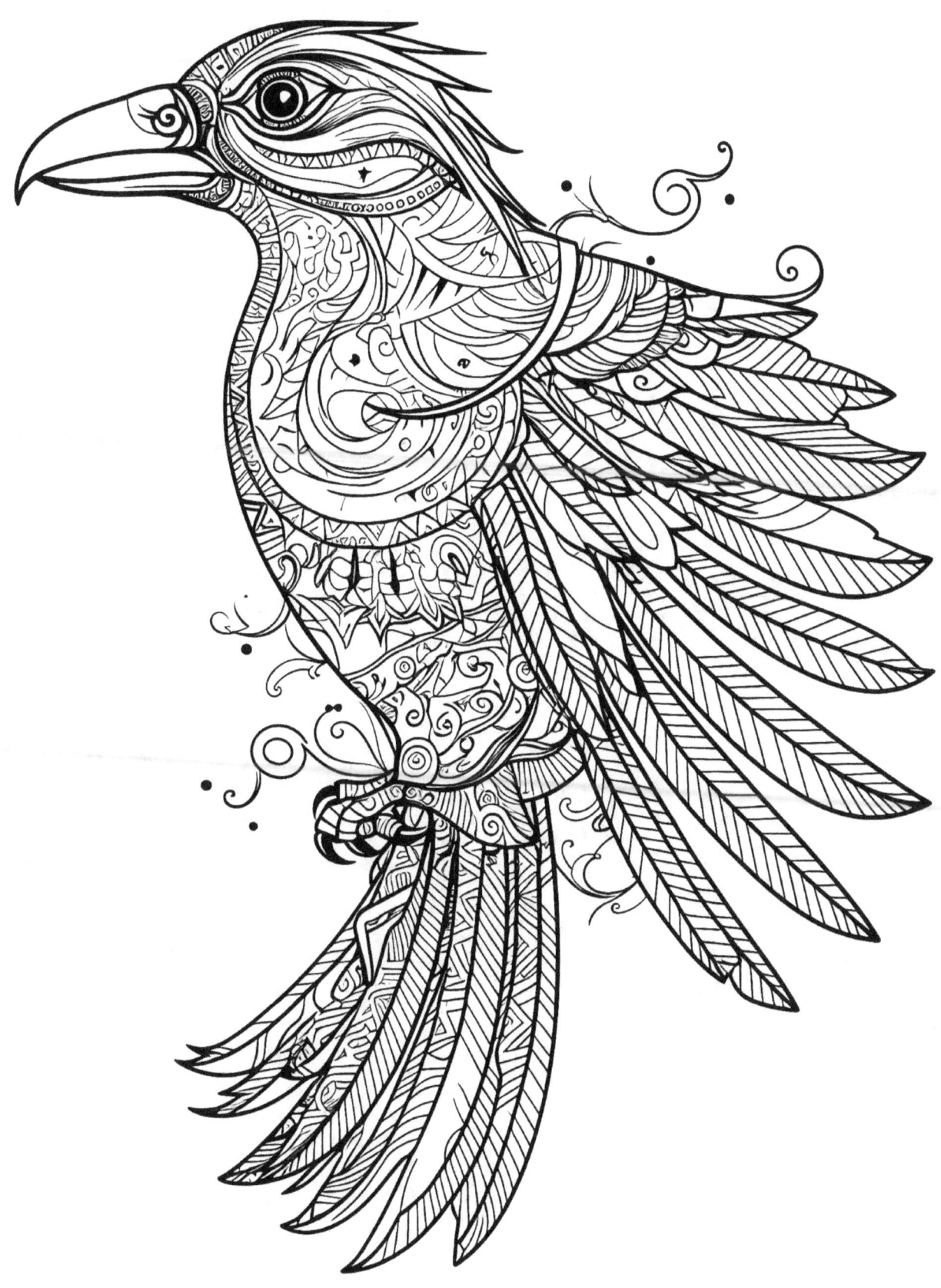

Rose

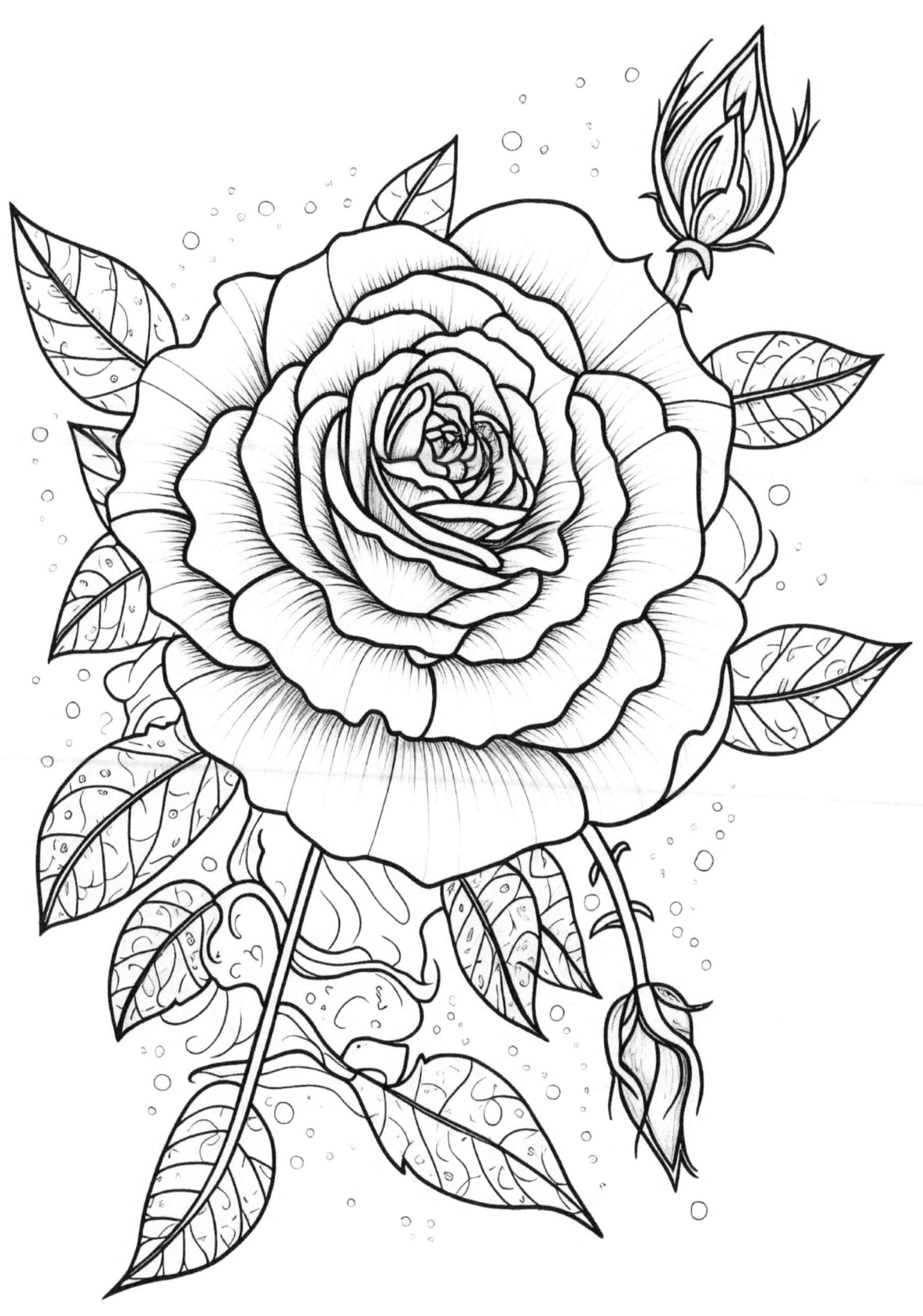

Skull

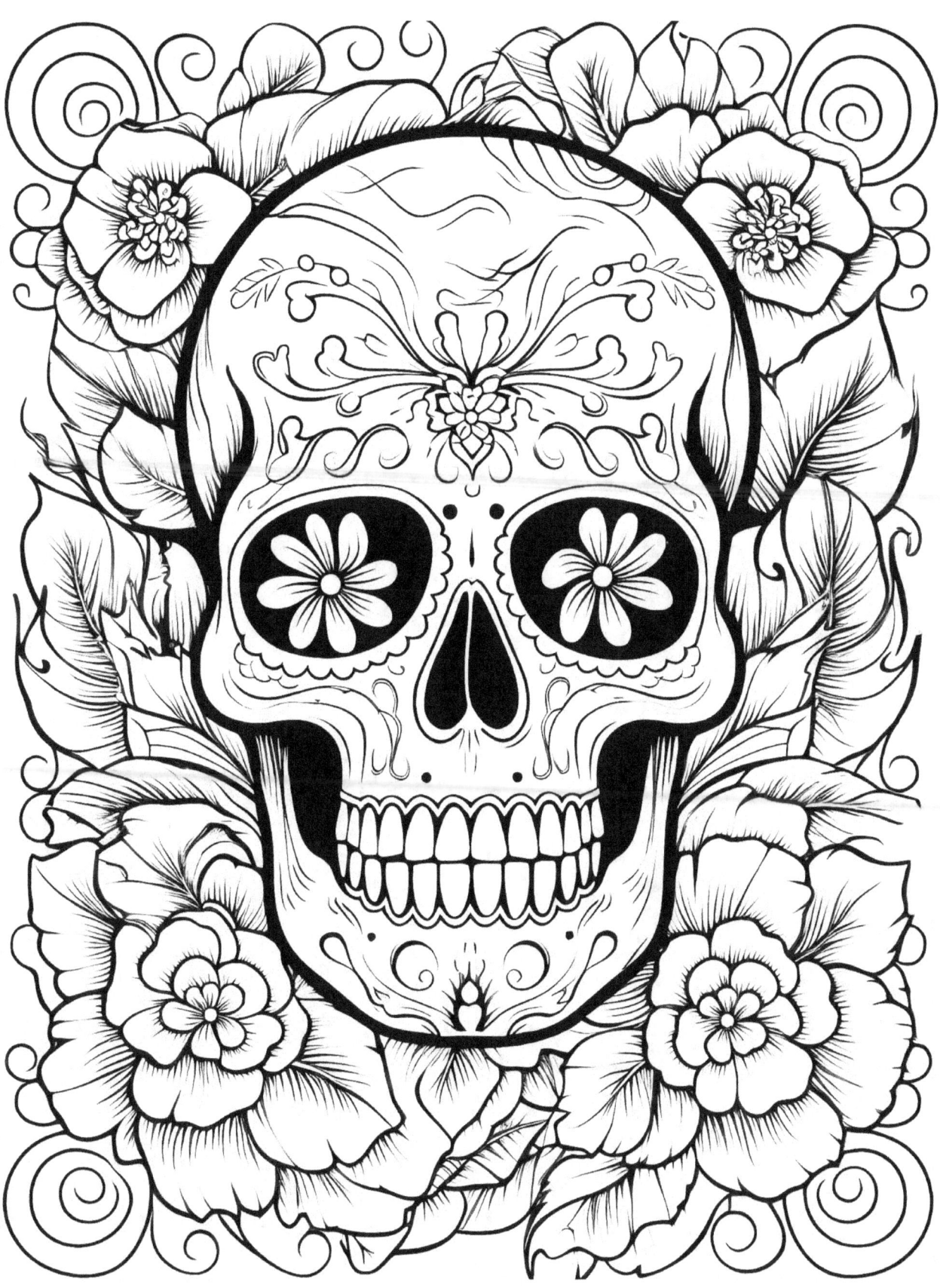

Skyline

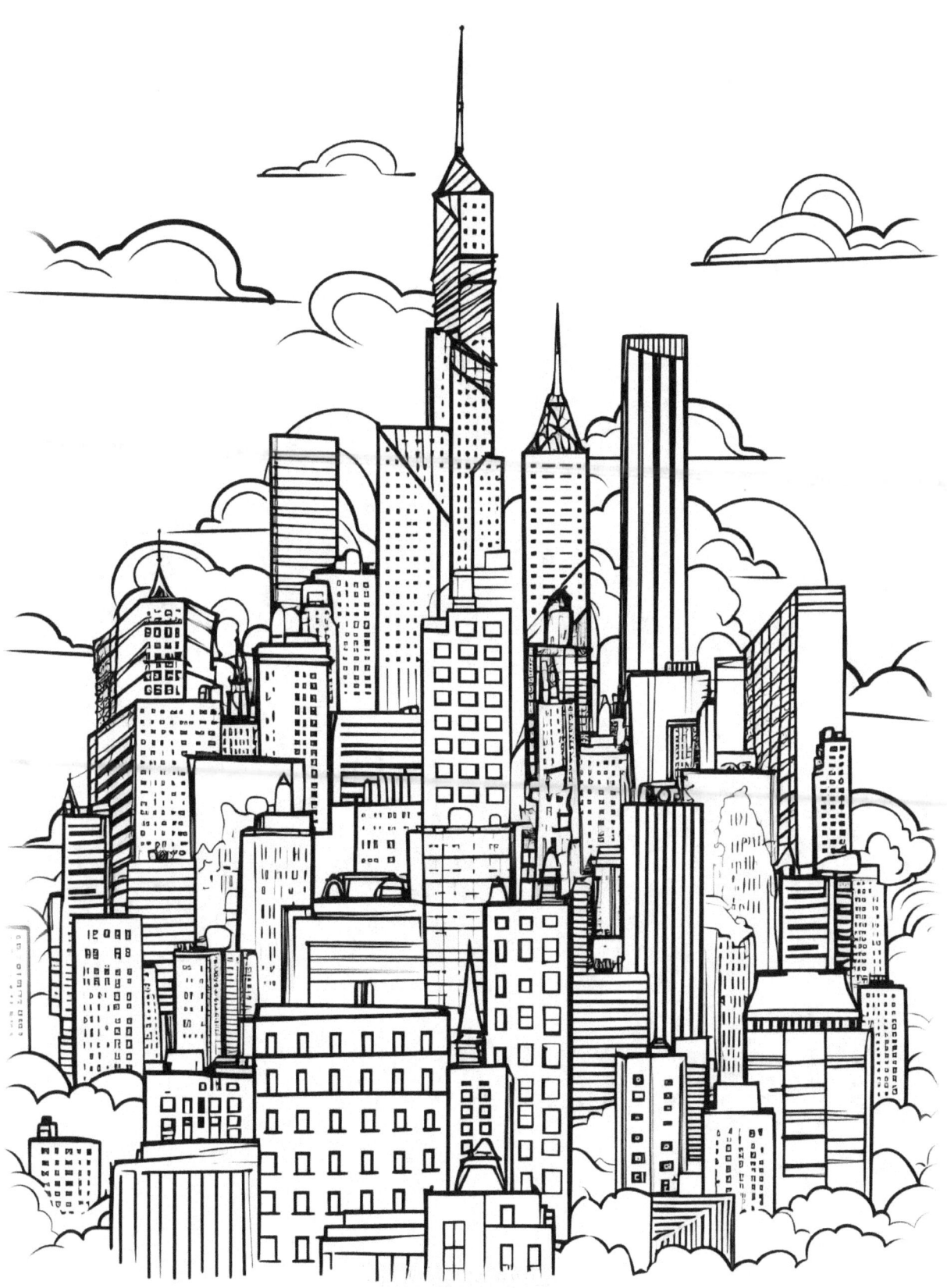

Snake

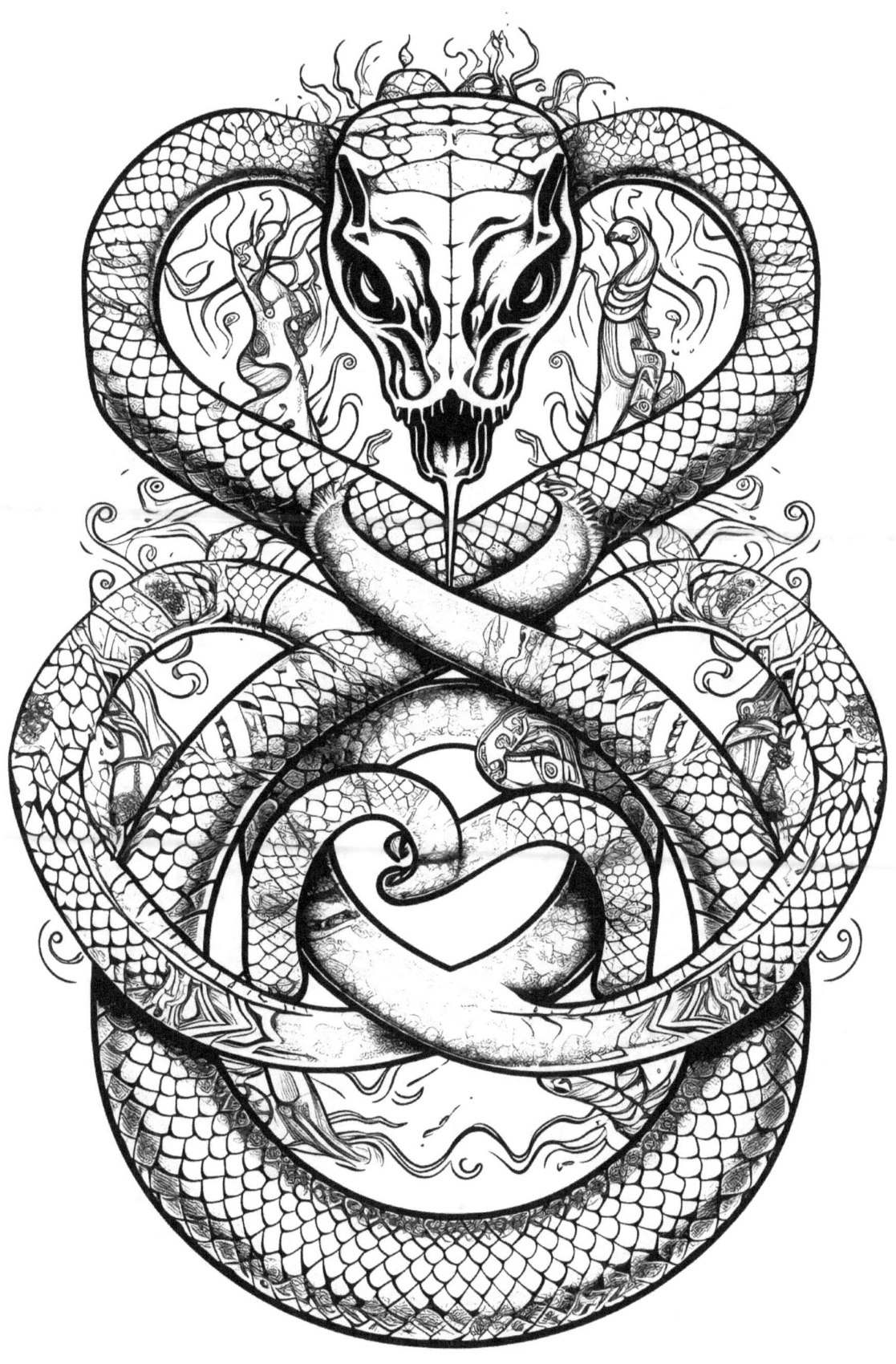

Star

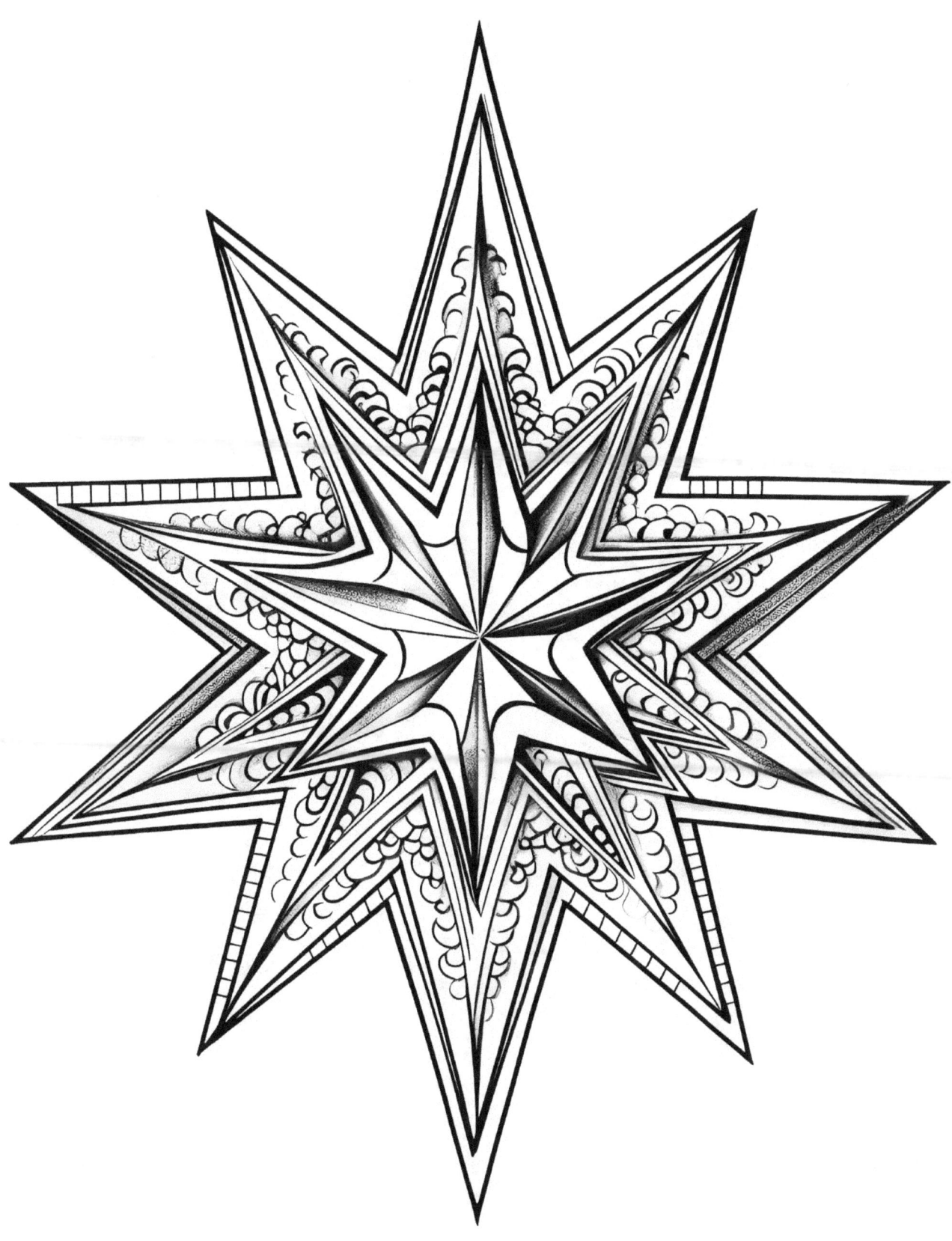

Sun and Moon

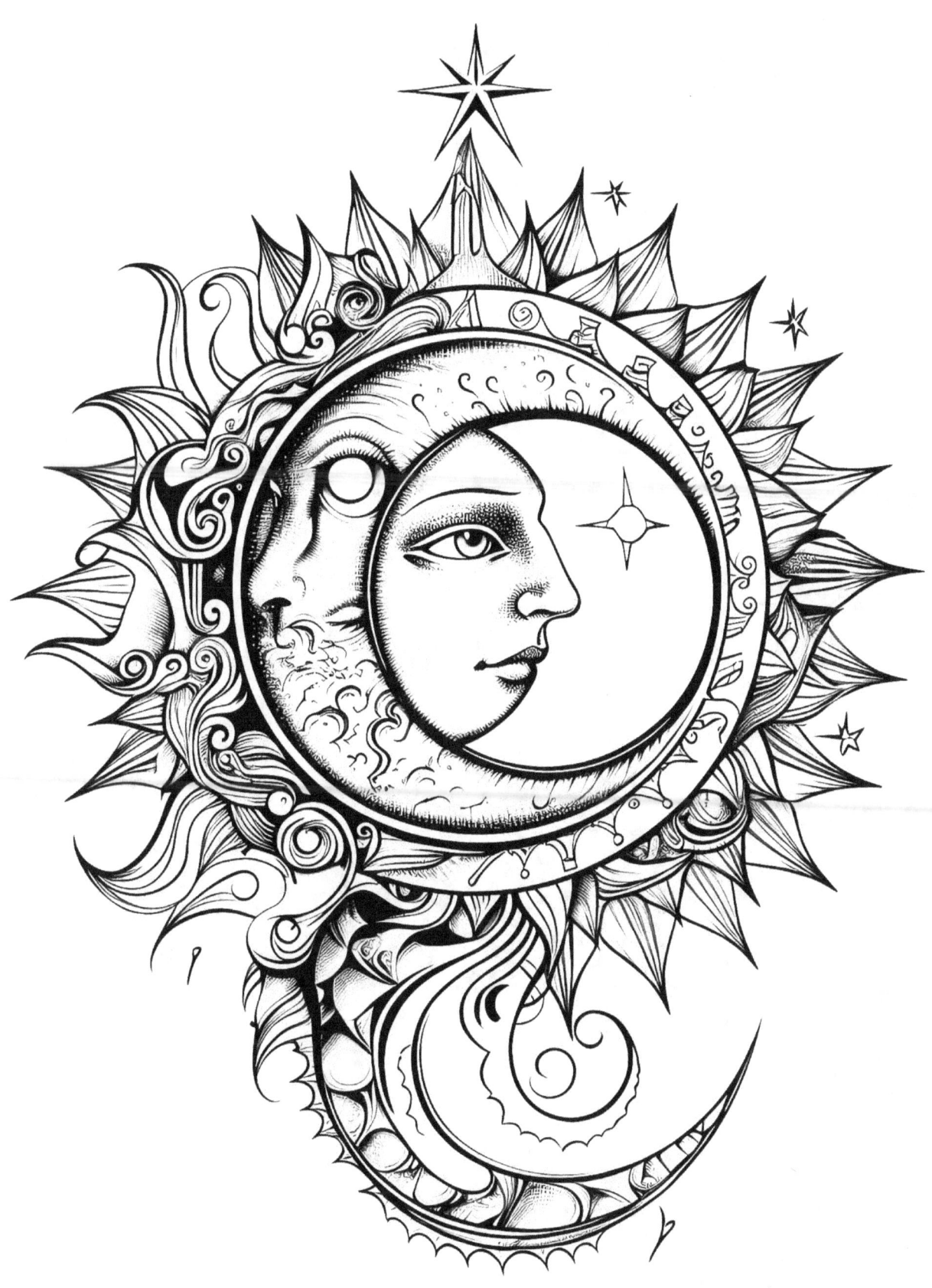

Sun

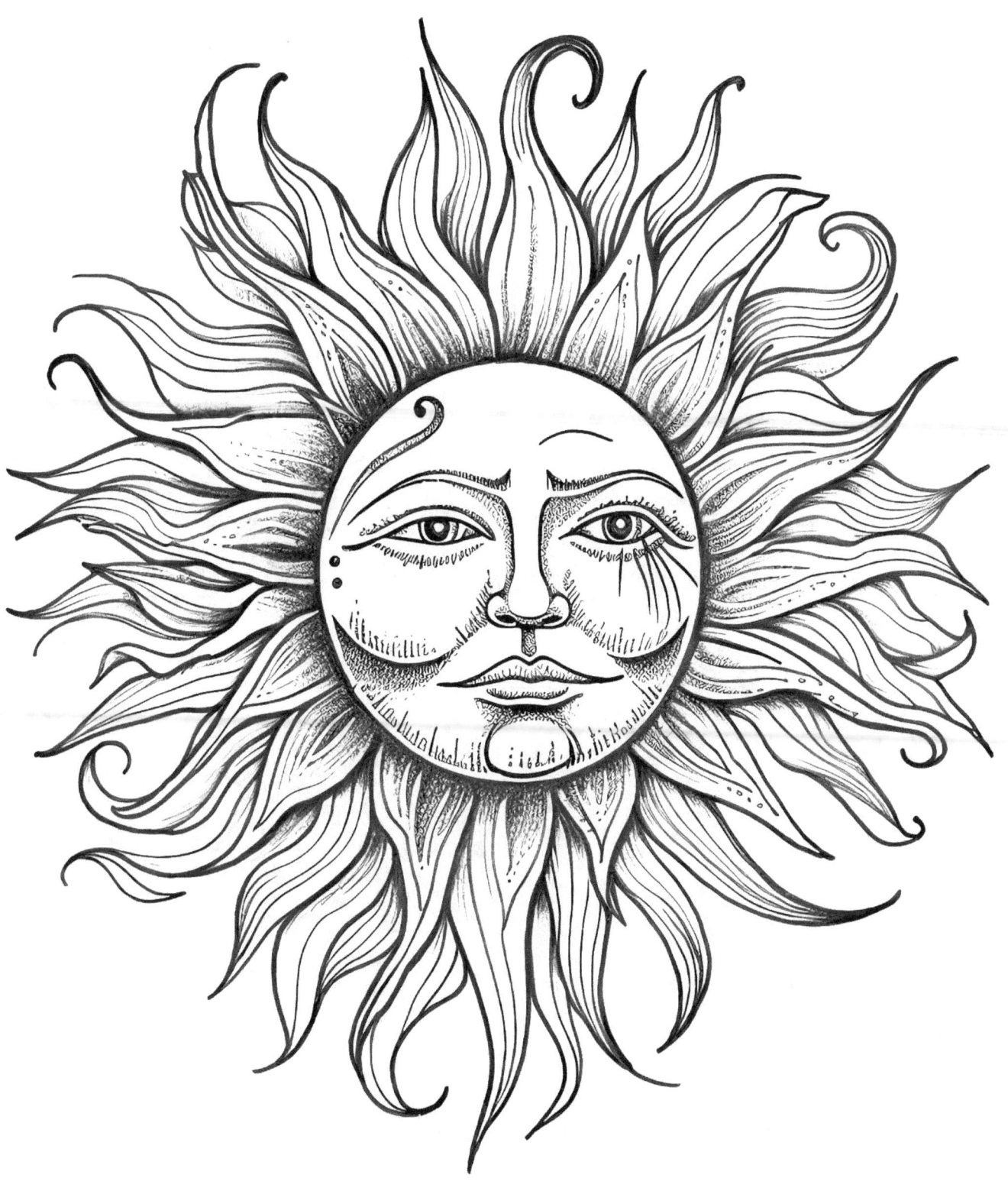

Tiger

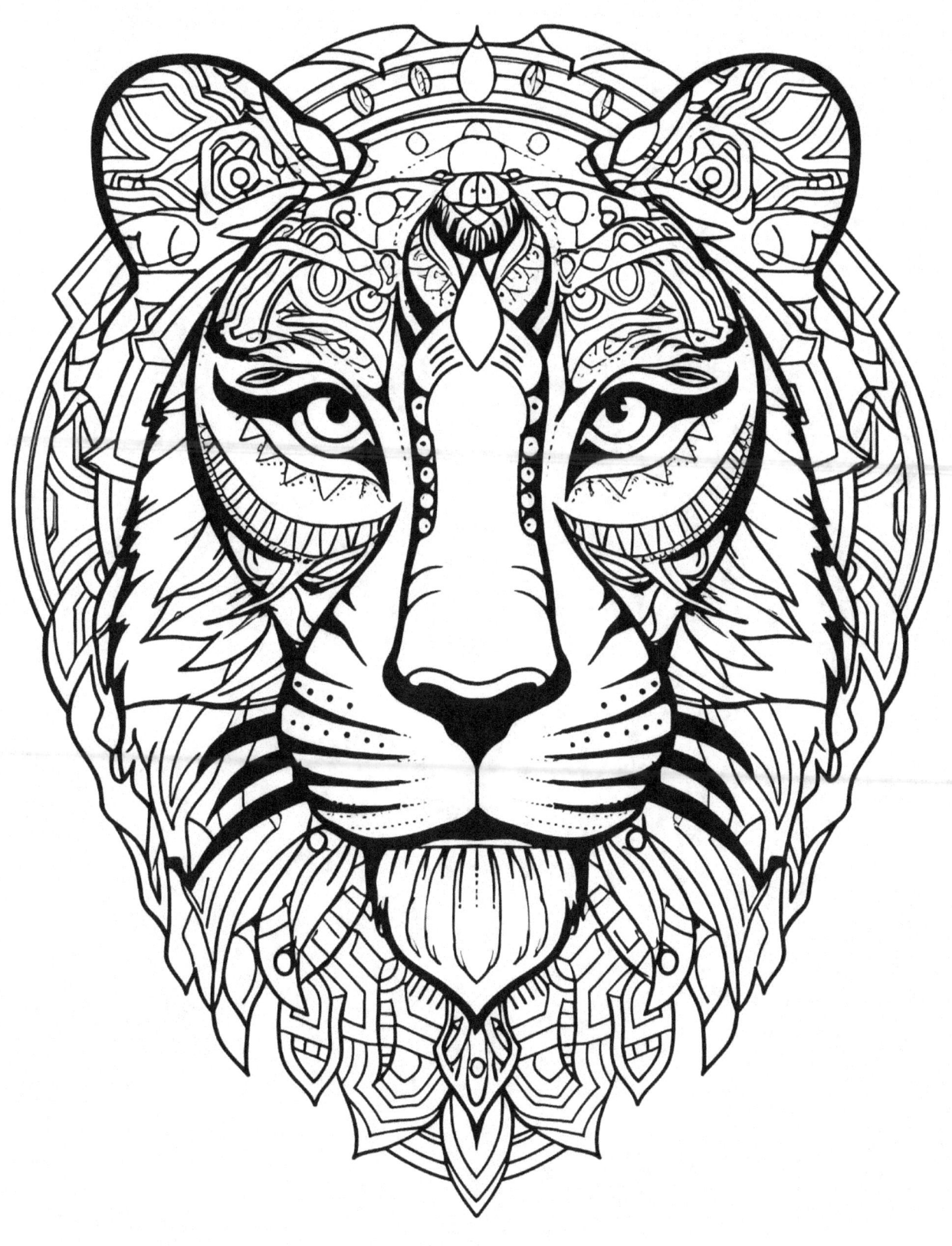

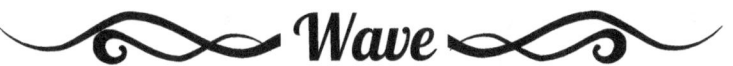

Wave

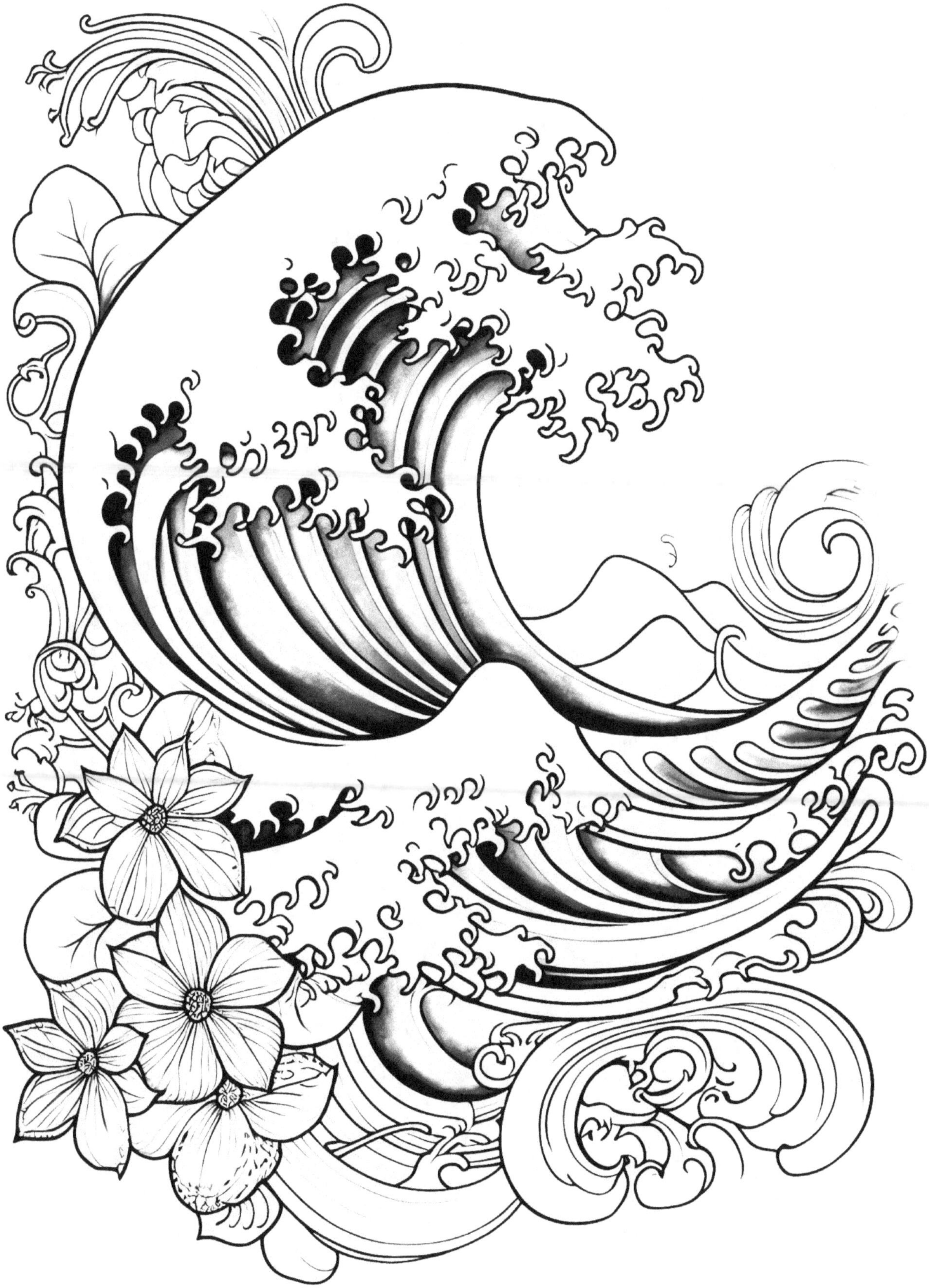

Wildflowers

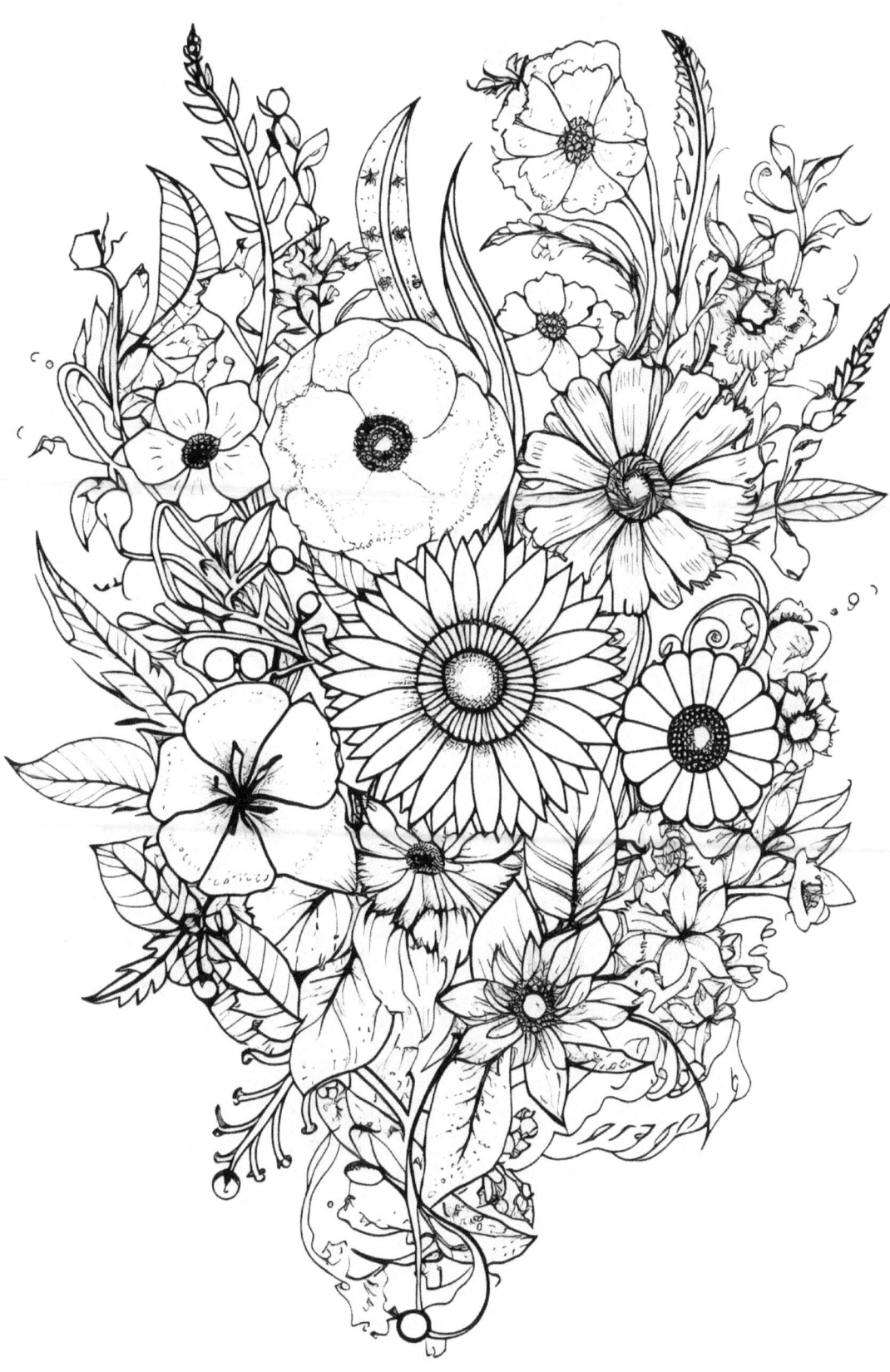

Wings

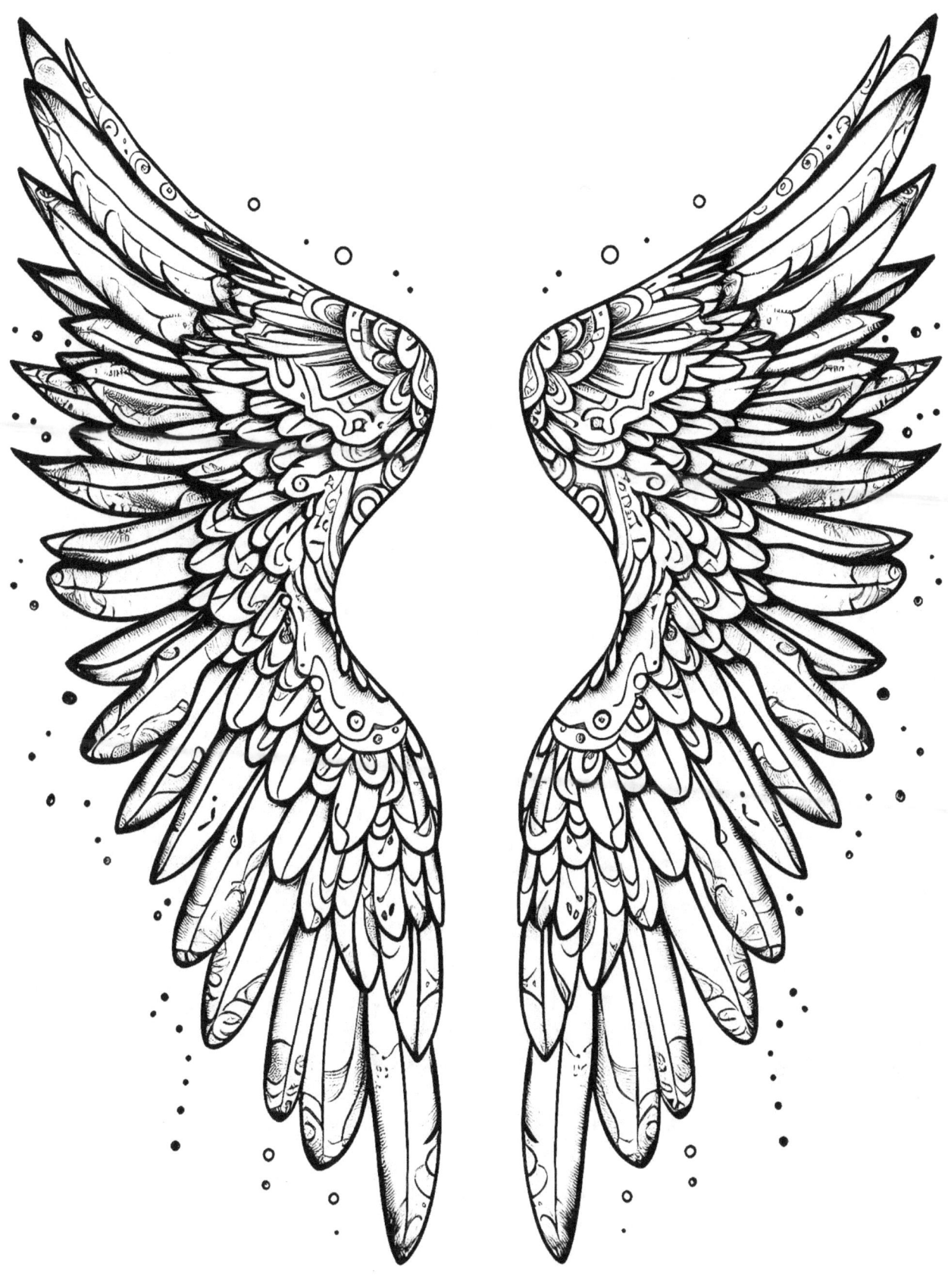

VISIT US ONLINE
to learn more about our
latest fun, family-friendly books
or search for us on Amazon.

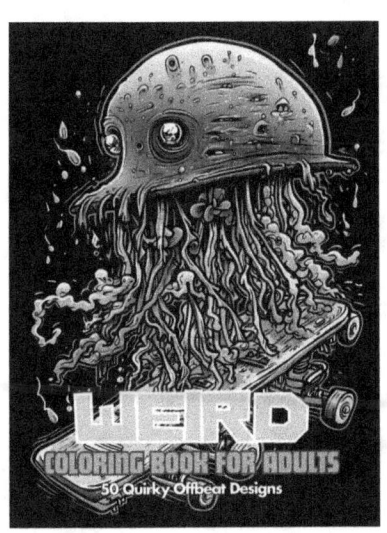
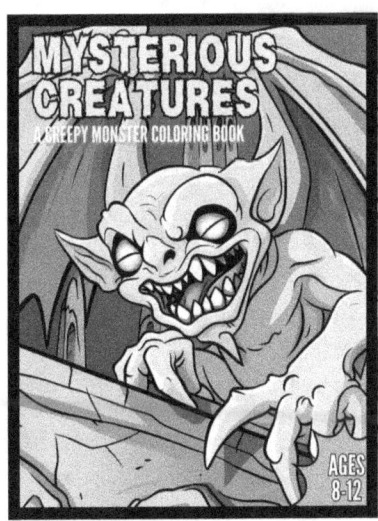
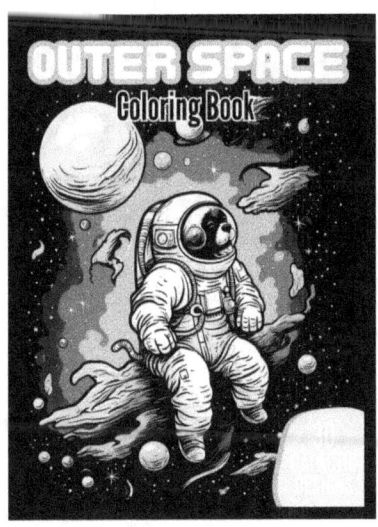

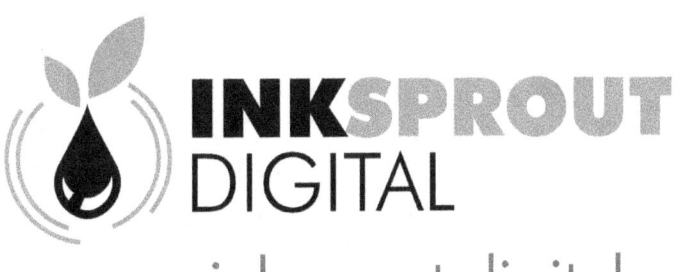

www.inksprout.digital